1000 LIMERICKS FOR KIDS

Joel Rothman

Illustrations by Heather Munro

WARD LOCK LIMITED · LONDON

First published in Great Britain in 1985
by Ward Lock Limited, 82 Gower Street,
London WC1E 6EQ.

Typeset in Times by Spire Print Services Limited, Salisbury, Wilts.
Printed and bound in Finland.

Reprinted 1985

British Library Cataloguing in Publication Data

Rothman, Joel
    1000 limericks.
    1. Limericks–Juvenile literature
    I. Title
    821'.07   PZ8.3

ISBN 0-7063-6349-3

Contents

By Way of Introduction

A limerick's a joke in verse,
Or even a moral (which is worse).
There's 1000 here
To fill you with cheer.
By the end, you'll be feeling quite terse.

A limerick, to be sure,
Should have five lines, no more.
But if you're slick, you can get away with six,
Whilst others require only four!

A limerick's meant to rhyme,
Generally all of the time.
But don't be a fool,
It's no hard and fast rule –
Not all of them must.

Mad Miscellany

A farmer's daughter from Chigwell
Knew how to hoe and to dig well.
When her father got ill,
She grabbed up the swill
And fed all the tiniest pigs well.

I know an old lady called Meg
So hard up she had to beg.
In one butcher's shop
She asked for a chop,
And pleaded for one chicken leg.

A man from Stockton-on-Tees
Produced phenomenal peas.
He then moved to Jarrow
And grew a green marrow
Too big to go in the deep-freeze.

There was a soldier called Hugh,
Who caused a hullabaloo
By baring his thigh,
Which read: 'I love Di' –
A military tattoo!

There was an old man in Iraq
Who lived in a tumbledown shack.
One day he struck oil,
While digging his soil;
And he now drives a gold cadillac!

There was a young man of Woking,
Who didn't enjoy a soaking.
When told that real fellas
Don't use umbrellas,
He said, 'Why, you've got to be joking.'

There was a young man of Japan
Who wrote verse that never would scan.
When they said 'But the thing
Doesn't go with a swing,'
He said 'Yes but I always like to get as many words into the
    last line as I possibly can!

There was a man named Jason
Who trained to be a mason;
And one of his tips
Was, 'Catch all the chips
Then fry them in a deep basin.'

I know a dry old stick
Whose wit is really quick.
He's been going to plays
Since Edwardian days,
And calls himself 'Old Vic'!

All that the audience views
Of the readers on *The Nine O'Clock News*
Is the smart upper half,
But it might prove a laugh
If we saw their down-at-heel shoes.

It rained when we went to see *Jaws*,
And we stood in a queue out of doors.
The weather was wet,
And wet *we* did get;
It never just rains, it pours!

There was a young man of Kuwait
Who was late and just couldn't wait.
He complained to the waiter,
Who said, 'I'll come later
To wait on you, so you must wait.'

There's a place in Wales called Mumbles,
Filled with groans and with grumbles.
The locals complain
Of constant cold rain,
Which produces a coastline that crumbles.

There was a faith-healer from Keele,
Who said, 'Though pain isn't real,
If I sit on a pin
And it punctures my skin,
I don't like what I fancy I feel.'

My cousin's a high class lawyer,
Who's so snobbish he'll likely ignore yer;
If he starts to speak
As he did all last week,
He's certainly goin' to bore yer.

A teacher from Leamington Spa
Said to her pa and her ma,
'A boy whom I taught
Is a brave astronaut –
I said one day he'd go far!'

The modern delivery man
Arrives in a very smart van.
But some years ago,
As we old ones know,
The errand boys all simply ran.

There was a young lady from Delaware,
Who was most undoubtedly well aware
That to dress for a masque
Wasn't much of a task;
But she cried, 'What the heck will my fella wear?'

There was a young fellow of Acre,
Who took off his hat to a Quaker;
When the worthy man said,
'You are very well-bred',
He replied, 'Of course, I'm a baker.'

A well-dressed murderer, Jock,
Laid his head on the chopping block.
He was seen to frown
As the axe came down,
'Cause he'd noticed a hole in his sock.

A boy who can't stand the light
Only goes out when it's night.
He said to his dad,
'I know that you're sad
But everyone can't be so bright.'

When you think of the hosts without number
Who are slain by the deadly cucumber,
It's quite a mistake
Of such food to partake –
It results in a permanent slumber.

There was a young girl called Bella,
Who lived rather like a cave-dweller.
She travelled around
By underground,
And owned her own flat in a cellar.

I went to the greyhound track,
And saw an odd dog in the pack.
I hollered and bawled:
'How can it be called
A greyhound when it is so black?'

There was a young boy named Matt,
Who lived with his mum in a flat.
When they moved to a house
They spotted a mouse –
So now they both live with a cat.

There was a young man at the Ritz
Whose bill reduced him to fits.
He said: '90p
For a small cup of tea?
There's not even any free bits.'

A naughty girl named Flo
Wanted her knickers to show.
She wore a skirt
As short as a shirt,
And kept on bending down low.

There was a young man called Murray
Who tried to drive a big lorry.
He caused quite a fuss
When he smashed a school bus,
And never did say he was sorry!

There was a young man of London
Who found he was being shunned on,
For he used the names
Of society dames
To limerick and sometimes to pun on.

A Frenchman named Pierre
Directed the *Folies Bergere*.
With a small bit of greenery,
And no other scenery,
The stage looked curiously bare!

There was a young boy called Tod
Who wasn't a rocker or mod.
To his Mum's great relief,
His only belief
Was that plaice was far better than cod.

All the guests at the animal fair
Had to dress up before they went there.
My friend, Eddy Brian,
Dressed up like a lion –
But I went in the nude, as a bear!

There was a young man named Steve
Whose behaviour was hard to believe:
He'd never say 'please',
Or beg pardon to sneeeze;
And he'd shine up his shoes on your sleeve!

An excitable girl called Camille
At the fair-ground is likely to squeal.
She made a loud sound
As she spun round and round,
'Cause no one could stop the Big Wheel.

A fiery fellow named Paul
At the fun-fair had a real ball:
He pelted his mates
With cups and with plates,
At the crockery-smashing stall.

I know of a bellboy called Robby
Who has a disgusting hobby.
Some think that he's nuts,
'Cause he saves all the butts
That he finds on the floor in the lobby!

There was a young man named Rod
Who ate his peas from the pod,
Consumed fish from the shell,
And drank water from the well –
Which was most exceedingly odd.

An impetuous fellow called Tim,
Who often did things on a whim,
Painted his head
White, blue and red,
After getting a Yul Brynner trim.

There was an old man called Stan,
Who put his foot in a pan
Of mustard and water,
Then got his young daughter
To cool off his face with a fan.

An Irish builder called Taffy
Was most assuredly daffy.
For he built abodes
Where there were no roads,
And opened a transport cafe!

I know a girl called Hortense,
Who is uncommonly dense.
Her body is big
'Cause she eats like a pig,
But her brain is not so immense.

An old man from way out in Bicester
Was walking one day with his sister,
When a bull with one poke
Tossed her into an oak –
But that old guy never missed her.

A bull in a china shop
Made the shopkeeper blow his top.
For this giant wild bison
Was breaking the Meissen,
And no one could make it stop.

There once was a boy called Louis,
Who constantly ate something chewy.
If he ran out of sweets,
He'd chew on his teeth –
His dental decay's quite untruey!

A hungry young man of Athlone
Had every reason to moan.
His wife ate the ham
And a thick leg of lamb,
So all that was left was the bone.

There is an old man called Fred
Who makes his own cakes and bread.
When he cooks a pancake,
It's not a fake,
'Cause it really is made from lead!

A senile old man named Saul
Saw some boys playing football.
He tried to partake –
Which was a mistake,
For he dribbled and started to crawl.

A practical designer, Bess,
Made her very own dress
From black-and-white squares –
Now people in pairs
Can hire her chest to play chess!

A strapping young man named Howard,
Is reputed to be muscle-powered.
But when a mouse
Crept into his house
He jumped on the table – the coward!

A practical joker from Neath
Filed to a point his front teeth.
Intending to fright,
He exposed them at night
To joggers upon Hampstead Heath.

When showing his wisteria,
A gardener got hysteria,
For he was told
That a marigold
Was very much superior.

The gardens of elegant Kew
Are certainly nothing new.
Her majesty Queen Anne
Submitted the plan
To dig them, in 1702.

There was a kid named Sid
Who lived in Spanish Madrid.
The things that he did,
This kid from Madrid,
To know you must pay me a quid!

There was a girl called Winnie
Who was a bit of a ninny.
She made a mess
All down her dress,
And wished she'd worn her pinny.

The was a young girl from Rangoon,
Who danced by the light of the moon.
She had breakfast in bed,
And slept, it is said,
Well into the late afternoon.

Thirty days have September,
April, June and November.
Most of the others have thirty-one:
An extra day to have some fun!

At a restaurant in Long Drayton,
A vegetarian was quite shaken
When the waitress said:
'There's no eggs or bread,
But I've managed to save you some bacon.'

I know an old lady called Sybil
Who likes the odd snack, just to nibble.
If she doesn' get
It, you can sure bet
It, won't be too long till she'll dribble.

There was a young lady called Molly
Who liked her Christmases jolly.
Her mistletoe bough
Was really a wow,
And in all the beds she'd put holly.

I went to a smashing fair,
And smashed a piano there.
Black notes and white
Flew all through the night,
And some strings got caught in my hair.

A nervous old lady named Clair
Detected strange sounds in the air,
When she heard a big roar
Outside her front door,
She trembled and shook with great fear.

A certain young girl called Tess
Is in one hell of a mess,
For naughty Nelly
Put lots of red jelly
All over her new party dress.

A newborn baby, Lou,
Grew and grew and grew,
And grew and grew
And grew and grew,
And grew and grew and grew!

When crossing the Irish Sea,
A sailor confided in me,
'We're turning back
To Dublin, Jack,
For the captain wants t' pee.'

An amorous girl called Kate
Was told she'd have to wait
For the fruit of the palm,
But she learned with alarm
That her wait makes her late for a date.

There is a young lady of Lancs,
Who's as thick as two wooden planks.
In fact she's so dense,
She once changed ten pence
For one shilling, and then she said, 'Thanks'.

A conceited young boy called Bob,
Was commonly known as a snob.
When asked to make tea,
He'd say, 'No, not me,
That's certainly not my job!'

I know a man named Dave,
Who's handsome, kind and brave.
This handsome Dave,
Of whom I rave,
Is in the mirror when I shave.

A wild young man and his horse
Full of bravado and sauce,
Tried to jump over
The white cliffs of Dover,
But couldn't quite muster the force.

There was a young girl named Michelle
Whot fancied herself as a swell.
She took her friend Alice
Along to the Palace,
And rang on the front doorbell!

A conceited young man called Doug
Is unbelievably smug.
In bed at night
He'll turn down the light
And give himself a big hug!

A silly young girl named Fiona
Was oh such a moaner and groaner.
One day in despair
She pulled out her hair –
Soon after, no man would dare phone her.

Happy birthday to you!
Squashed tomatoes and stew;
Bread and butter in the gutter,
Happy birthday to you!

> A carpenter called Miles
> Always wears wide smiles.
> He gets call after call
> To fit mats wall to wall,
> And he's certainly making thick piles!

There was an explorer named Janet
Who flew to a far-away planet.
Upon her return
We all grew to learn
That the planet was one mass of granite!

> There is a paper-boy called Mike
> Whose uphill round is like a hike.
> He loses pounds
> On all his rounds,
> Because he doesn't have a bike.

There was a young man from Bristol
Who owned a dangerous pistol.
Just for fun
He fired the gun,
And shattered a vase of pure crystal.

> Men with bells on cords
> Have to wake the hoards
> Of dreaming dukes
> In ermine suits –
> This is the House of Lords!

There once was a young lad named Hugh
Who when given soft eggs said, 'Pooh!
Take it out of my sight,
I can't stand the white,
It's a horrible mess of goo!'

> There is a woman called Clair
> Whose head is completely bare.
> She stays in her home
> To polish her dome.
> Hairdressers say, 'That's not fair!'

An eager young fellow called Clive
Thrust his hand into a beehive.
He said, 'There's big money
In stealing wild honey –
I've been doing it since I was five.'

> There is a young laddie called Robin,
> Who's usually sighin' and sobbin'.
> His eyes are less tearful,
> His manner's more cheerful,
> Whenever he rides on a Dobbin.

There was a young girl called Lottie
Whose face was inclined to be spotty.
That wasn't so bad,
But what was more sad –
Her brain was decidedly dotty.

There was a naughty old friar
Who had to report to the prior.
The prior told Tuck,
'You've run out of luck –
I've just spied you smoking a briar.'

A venerable archdeacon
Announced that he would speak on
The care of flowers
For hours and hours –
A sermon he'll spend a whole week on!

I have a motoring friend
Who drives me round the bend.
He's not a chap
To use a map –
We drove right past Land's End!

A boy who dressed up as a page
For a wedding, was in a great rage.
He said, 'What a farce –
I feel like an arse,
I might as well be on the stage.'

A teacher whose name is Jim Kerm,
Loves fishing with hook, rod and worm.
Whilst working he's wishing
To be outdoors fishing –
He'll go at the end of term.

A boy by the first name of Thomas
Loved looking at all the tall llamas.
In the zoo he would stare
At the ones they had there,
And think of his furry pyjamas.

There was a man named Hanick,
A very smart mechanic.
When he was in bed
He studied and read,
And soon what he knew was titanic.

What's in a name

There once was a boy called Strong,
But he wasn't a child who was strong.
Just to lift up
A small, brown pup
Took Strong the whole day long.

I know a fellow named Will,
Who objects to being called Bill.
His behaviour is silly
If called 'Billy' or 'Willy';
And 'William' makes him feel ill.

One bright and warm sunny day,
A man went to rest in some hay.
When asked, 'Are you hot?',
He said, 'I am not –
My name is Willy Mackay.'

There once was a Tyrannosaurus,
Who lived when the earth was all porous.
But it fainted with shame
When it first heard its name,
And departed the earth long before us.

There once was a Roman, Ignatius,
Who met a man called Horatius.
Said Ig, 'Our names
Both end the same.'
Said Horace, 'So they do, good gracious!'

Have you heard of the Greek called Homer?
Well, his name is quite a misnomer.
He was never at home;
He travelled to Rome
And should have been christened 'The Roamer'!

There was a young man of Karachi,
Who was commonly known as Archie.
But now he is called,
In full, Archibald.
He's married and now he's turned starchy.

There was a young girl called Clarise
Who liked to be called 'Miss Harris';
Or 'Sweet Mam'selle'
Would please her quite well,
If ever she went to see Paris.

Tongue twisters

There was an old dame of Dunbar,
Who took the 4.4 to Forfar,
But it went on to Dundee,
So she travelled, you see,
Too far by 4.4 from Forfar.

A tutor who taught on the flute,
Tried to teach two young tooters to toot.
Said the two to the tutor:
'Is it harder to toot, or
To tutor two tooters to toot?'

An earnest young fisherman, Fisher,
Once fished from the edge of a fissure.
A fish with a grin
Pulled the fisherman in –
Now they're fishing the fissure for Fisher!

There once was a writer named Wright,
Who instructed his son to write right.
He said, 'Son, write Wright right.
It is not right to write
Wright as 'rite' – try to write Wright aright!'

A flea and a fly in a flue,
Were trapped, so they thought, 'What to do?'
'Let us fly,' said the flea,
'Let us flee,' said the fly,
So they flew through a flaw in the flue!

A man called William S. Bugbee
Once said to a bed-bug, 'Don't bug me.'
The bed-bug told Bugbee,
'Please sit here and hug me –
'Cos I'm deathly afraid that you'll mug me.'

If you catch a chinchilla in Chile,
And then cut off its beard, willy-nilly,
With a small razor-blade,
You can say that you've made
A Chilean chinchilla's chin chilly.

Nutty Nursery Rhymes

There was a young girl named Jill
Who said to Jack, 'You're quite ill!
It's so absurd,
Who ever heard
Of a well on the top of a hill?'

Hickory-dickory-dock,
The mouse ran up the clock.
From deep inside
A cuckoo cried:
'At least you ought to knock.'

Four-and-twenty blackbirds
Baked in a pie?
Anyone who eats it
Is sure to sing and fly!

'Mary, Mary, quite contrary,
How does your garden grow?'
'Wilder and wilder,
As the weather gets milder;
It's quite full of weeds, don't you know.'

Little Jack Horner

Little Jack Horner
Scored in the corner
A perfectly wonderful try.
It came from a plum
Of a pass from the scrum –
Said he, 'What a great star am I.'

Little Jack Horner
Sat in a corner,
Eating a piece of pie.
He rubbed his tum
And said to his mum,
'Is this the best you can buy?'

Little Jack Horner
Went to a sauna
And found the temperature hig
He said to his mum,
'I've burnt my bum –
I hope you've not burnt the pie

Little Jack Horner
Sat in a corner
Eating a piece of cake.
He spat out a crumb
And said to his mum:
'You ought to learn how to bak

The Queen of Heart's Tarts

The Queen of Hearts
Baked some tarts
Over an open fire.
The King then spoke,
'These taste of smoke.'
Said she, 'You're a dirty liar!'

Little Miss Muffet
Sat on her tuffet
Eating delicious tarts;
She's now up in court,
Because it is thought
They belonged to the Queen of Hearts.

Humpty Dumpty sat on a wall,
To get a good view over all.
Some thought him super,
Others, a snooper;
I think he was pushed – did he fall?

Little Bo-peep's Sheep

Little Bo-peep
Has lost her flock,
And doesn't know where to find them,
Because she went
To change her frock,
And left her brother to mind them.

Little Bo-peep has lost her sheep
And I know where to find them:
In the deep-freeze,
With packs of peas
Stacked up neatly behind them.

Mary loves strawberry jam
And cream as white as snow:
She puts them on her doughnuts,
And does her waistline grow!

Little Miss Muffet
Sat on her tuffet
Eating chicken and chips:
Her sister who's hateful,
Ate half the plateful,
Then strolled away licking her lips.

Little Lord Fauntleroy
Was thoroughly spoilt and coy.
His velvet suit
Was quite a beaut,
But, yuk, what a horrible boy!

Little Boy Blue
Come blow on your tuba;
The next three numbers
Are rhumbas from Cuba.

Little Miss Pocket
Sat on a rocket
And rode to the Milky Way.
Along came a Martian
(Rather a mean one),
Who made her pay just to stay.

Little Bo-peep has lost her sheep;
It's hard for her to slumber.
To bed she'll creep,
And try counting sheep,
But she'll usually get the wrong number.

A Sporting Chance

A racing driver called Neil
Went crazy behind the car wheel.
He drove his new Rover
From Brands Hatch to Dover,
And into the sea just past Deal.

A motorist called Sally
Doesn't dilly-dally.
She entered for fun,
And finally won,
The Monte Carlo Rally!

A woman who wasn't too stunning,
Competed in marathon running.
She really enjoys
Being chased by the boys.
Is she sporting, or really quite cunning?

A runner from Surrey called Gordon,
Whilst running a race was roared on
By many supporters,
And all of their daughters,
From Malden, Merton and Morden.

A girl with her hair in a bun,
Entered a marathon run.
It slowly unravelled
The further she travelled,
So she let down her hair – and won!

A runner from New Orleans
Lives entirely on fresh greens.
He moves with great speed,
And keeps in the lead,
'Cause he's stuffed with runner beans!

A dimwit with a javelin
Says he's still unravellin'
How to throw
And how to know
Which way the javelin's travellin'!

There once was a judge called Sir James
Who presided at the Olympic Games.
When he ruled out a high jump,
They gave him a hard thump
And called him some scandalous names.

There was a young athlete of Dorking
Who did a great deal of walking.
Her coach named Ted
Approvingly said,
'You're better off walking than talking.'

A golfer now out on the links,
Stops play at each tee for drinks.
Take it from me,
The drink isn't tea,
But a cocktail they call 'Hi Jinx'!

A certain golfer at Troon
Went off to the course at noon.
His shots went astray,
Right off the fairway –
He's playing still, under the moon.

I'm sorry for those poor souls
Who give up golf for bowls.
They roll a ball
And that is all,
For the greens have got no holes!

There was a young golfer called Clive
Who had dedication and drive.
But inflation he claimed,
Was ruining his game –
Where he used to shout 'fore' now its 'five'.

Now handball's a wonderful sport,
But near me there's no proper court.
So I smack the black ball
Against my hall wall,
Which makes my neighbour quite fraught.

A certain young man of Frinton,
Who rejoiced in the name of Clinton,
Wasn't too subtle
When hitting a shuttle:
They said he played only *bad*-minton.

My little brother Dennis
Really is a menace.
He shouted 'Let'
And lowered the net,
Which isn't cricket – or tennis!

A cricketer in Penzance
Bats with a peculiar stance.
His pads are strapped,
So his legs are trapped
In only one side of his pants.

A cricketer of considerable fame,
Dishonestly earned his acclaim.
By cheating at cricket
And glueing his wicket,
He'd always win all of his games.

There once was a great big black cat,
Who swallowed a whole cricket bat;
He swallowed the ball,
The stumps, bails and all –
So the cricket team clobbered him flat!

I know a man called Dai
Who'd like what money can't buy:
To play for Wales
And tell true tales
Of how he scored a try!

A lad on a football team
Worked out a tactical scheme.
He and his mates,
Together scored eight –
The lad then awoke from his dream.

A young man from Istanbul
Was certainly nobody's fool.
'As a football fan,'
Says he, 'You can
Support only Liverpool.'

Fishermen and footballers get
Plenty of sport, you can bet.
Whether it's a goal
Or a big Dover sole,
They'll shout: 'It's now in the net!'

An unlucky fisherman's mate
Said over his empty plate,
'There's no food honey,
'Cause I've no money –
You spent it all on the bait.'

A yachtswoman from Cowes
Wears a loose-fitting blouse.
With just half a gale,
It's as good as a sail
If she stands up straight in the bows.

There was a swimmer from Sale
Who was hit on the nose by a whale.
It happened at Rhyl –
Said he, 'What a thrill,
I'm still living to tell the tale.'

There was a young bather named Mark
Who saw the fin of a shark.
He said, 'This deep sea
Is no place for me –
I'll swim in the lake at the park!

A young man called Rodney Brace,
Who competed in a swimming race,
Was disqualified
When a judge spied,
A motor to quicken his pace.

A fellow who's quite short and stocky
May well end up being a jockey.
If he doesn't like horses,
The answer of course is
To take up snooker or hockey.

An aggressive young man from Tring
Thinks that snooker is just the thing.
He used his cue
With such follow-through
That now his arm's in a sling.

Enterprising

There was a young craftsman called Steve
Who much, by hard work, could achieve.
For hours he'd sit
And crochet and knit,
And even embroider and weave.

A man from Galashiels
Has done some clever deals.
From a borrowed pram
He sells bread and jam:
It's 'Kiddies' meals-on-wheels'!

A travelling salesman, Tobias,
Knocked on our door to sell us
A washing-machine
(The worst ever seen) –
And he also sold towels to dry us!

Money in County Kildare
Is always remarkably rare.
A financial martyr
Started to barter,
And opened a swap-shop there.

A bakery student named Jake,
Decided that he could make
A quick quid or two
If he married sweet Sue,
And charged her dad for the cake.

The man who invented the socket
Went on to develop the sprocket.
Then one afternoon,
He went to the moon.
That's right – he'd invented the rocket.

This is a tale of a gent,
Who fished with a pin that was bent.
He actually hooked,
And eventually cooked,
A flat Dover sole in Kent!

A one-legged man in a kilt
Had a special appliance built.
In Aberdeen
He can be seen
On a crutch and a tall, wooden stilt.

A thin-blooded man of Crete
Had a most peculiar sheet.
It was a deep red,
Had a hole for his head,
And two others just for his feet.

A fat, lazy girl called Jill
Lived on a hill near Brill.
She'd sit on a trolley
And open her brolly –
The wind blew her right up that hill.

An ingenious girl called Brenda
Asked her friend Jane to lend her
A small paper-clip
To hold up her slip,
And a pin for her broken suspender.

Most off-licences stock
A German white wine called hock,
But I don't buy a lot
'Cause grapes grow on my plot,
And I strain their juice through my sock.

There was a young lady of Malta,
Who strangled her aunt with a halter.
She said, 'I won't bury her,
She'll do for my terrier –
She'll keep for a month if I salt her.'

An acrobat called Uriah
Could cartwheel, and jump even higher.
He'd put on his wet clothes,
Spin round on his toes –
The very first tumble-drier!

A man who lives in a dell
Has an inspiring tale to tell.
With solid hard toil,
He bored deep for oil
Three times, and – well, well, well.

There was a young man called Dean,
Whose hair had a marvellous sheen.
It's dried in a tumble-drier;
No, I'm not a liar—
It makes his toupee extra clean!

A businessman named Shore
Owned a jewellry store.
The goods he sold
Were rings of gold:
I'm sure Shore wasn't poor.

Hall of Fame

An artist called Botticelli
Painted a model named Nelly
She slapped him, 'Take that,
You've painted me fat –
I'm slim and I've been on the telly.'

The author Thomas Hardy
Was rather lah-di-dah-di.
He'd say, if ever late
For a scheduled debate,
'Forgive me for being so tardy.'

A selfish composer was Handel,
Who caused a furious scandal:
When he saw a gorgon
Was playing his organ,
He set light to her hair with a candle.

The famous composer Liszt,
Was enraged and brought down his fist
On the piano keys,
So hard that he's
Just broken a bone in his wrist.

The composer Benjamin Britten,
Owned a musical kitten.
It played lovely tunes
On piano and spoons,
Much better than Britten had written.

The Latin poet Horace,
Said to his girlfriend, Doris,
'Let Judas Iscariot
Have my old chariot,
For I'm buying myself a new Morris.'

A duel 'tween Regency rakes
May not have been for high stakes.
It's said that Lord Byron
Actually fired on
All but his closest of mates.

The poet named William Blake
Started to shiver and shake,
When a bold unicorn
Approached him at dawn
And asked him for biscuits or cake.

The famous astronomer, Halley,
Whose ambition was to dance in a ballet,
Did a *pas de deux*,
In a tutu of fur,
When his comet was seen near Spring Valley.

Did you ever hear of Caesar?
He wasn't a very bright geezer.
He ruined all his wine
(Which had tasted divine)
By storing it in a deep-freezer.

The ancient Greek, Achilles,
Gave his sailors the willies.
He lost his way
To old Pompeii,
And they all ended up in the Scillies.

A lady named Catherine Howard
Was certainly not a coward.
With her head on the block
She continued to mock
Henry the Eighth – how she glowered.

It's said that George the First
Screamed and ranted and cursed,
Whenever his daughter
Spilled some of the water
She'd brought to slacken his thirst.

Napoleon Bonaparte
Had a tender heart.
His hand would rest
Upon his breast,
For fear it should depart.

When Hitler was Germany's boss,
He never seemed at a loss
To decorate
A Nazi mate,
With ribbon and Iron Cross.

The Seven Deadly Sins

God's plan made a hopeful beginning,
But man spoiled his chances by sinning.
We trust that the story
Will end in God's glory,
But at present the other side's winning!

Pride

The Queen put her sword by his head,
Then commanded, 'Arise – Sir Ted.'
Ted felt delighted
At just being knighted –
Good Lord, the Queen's cut off his head!

An arrogant child called Bart
Was just a little too smart.
His dad made him bend,
Then across his rear end
Bart learnt what it felt like to smart!

A clumsy girl of Chertsey
Was known as 'little Miss Flirtsy'.
When princes came 'round,
She'd fall to the ground
Trying to do a smooth curtsey.

Lust

A precious girl from Devon
Was in love at the age of seven.
When she gave up her toys
In favour of boys,
She discovered that they were like heaven!

A senile old man from West Broughton,
Fancied some females and sought 'em.
He'd often run after
The women with laughter,
But quite forgot why when he'd caught 'em!

A man who liked to philander,
Approached a young woman with candour.
All that she said
Was, 'Go and drop dead.'
Then struck him a mighty backhander.

There was a rich man named Link.
To every young woman he'd wink
And buy them things
Like diamonds and rings,
And very expensive, rare mink.

Anger

A Victorian lady named Alice
Gave vent to her feelings of malice –
She thought that the Queen
Could be terribly mean,
And so she threw stones at the Palace.

A man who enjoyed a bite,
Insisted his food be just right.
He scarred the cook
With a butcher's hook
When his meat was too tough one night.

A Welshman known as Dai
Threw a custard-pie
At Uncle Jack,
Who threw it back
Right into Dai's right eye.

There was a young man called Dick,
Who gave a hard kick to a brick.
Now what do you know –
Dick injured his toe,
And is hobbling around with a stick.

There once was a strong man named Russell,
Who became involved in a tussle.
But he soon lost face,
At a small seafood place,
When he struggled to open a mussel.

A captain yelled out with great force,
'Oh where, oh where is my horse?'
His men looked around,
But none could be found –
So the captain grew madder, of course.

Envy

A haughty, young man playing chess
Made his moves with the utmost finesse,
But he pondered his fate
When his friend shouted, 'Mate!
I've won and I'm thankful, God bless!'

Greed

There was a girl called Ada,
And did her mum upbraid 'er
For liking a bite
Right after midnight,
And being an ice-box raider!

A bilious blighter from Bude
Was sloppy, greedy and rude.
He'd fill his tum,
Then ask his mum,
'Have ya no' got any more food?'

An Italian, Valentino,
Whose appetite was obsceno,
Filled his belly
With vermicelli,
And several pints of red vino.

A famous grey mouse known as Mickey,
Was hungry and feeling quite picky.
He ate too much cheese,
Then hollered, 'Oh please
Get me a doctor – I'm sicky.'

There once was a fat boy called Kidd,
Who ate twenty pies for a quid.
When asked 'Are you faint?'
He replied, 'No, I ain't,
But I don't feel as well as I did!'

A greedy man from Rye
Just loved to eat apple-pie.
He sat on the floor
And ate forty-four,
Which caused that poor man to die.

There was an old man of Calcutta,
Who continually ate bread and butter
Till a big bit of muffin,
On which he was stuffin',
Choked that old man of Calcutta.

A fellow we knew called Keith
Died, so we sent him a wreath.
If you eat all day,
You're bound to lay
Dead, fed up to your teeth.

A greedy young girl called Jean
Swallowed a whole tangerine.
Her mother said, 'But
It should have been cut –
And besides it was unripe and so green.'

Covetousness

There was a young lad named Frank
Who wanted some fish from a tank.
As soon as he saw them,
He dived straight in for them;
But right to the bottom he sank!

Laziness

There was a young girl called Daisy –
Not smart, but not at all crazy.
Did she work? Not at all,
She was what you might call
Just clever enough to be lazy.

A lazy young man called Norman
Had a job as a part-time doorman.
His only quirk
Was to shirk all work,
So now he's just a poor man.

My lazy Uncle Mike
Welcomed the transport strike.
He stayed in bed,
'Can't walk,' he said,
'But you're welcome to borrow my bike.'

A girl called Anastasia
Could not have been any lazier.
She refused to clean brass
Or polish a glass –
She drove her mum crazier and crazier.

There was a princess, Amanda,
Whose subjects just couldn't stand 'er.
She'd put up her feet
In the midsummer heat,
Whilst servants stood over and fanned 'er!

There is an old man named Duggie,
Who rides everywhere in a buggy.
His feet just won't go
In rain or in snow,
And his legs grow supine when it's muggy.

There is a young man of Pinner,
Who has to prepare his own dinner.
He's not in the mood
To cook his own food,
So he's now getting thinner and thinner!

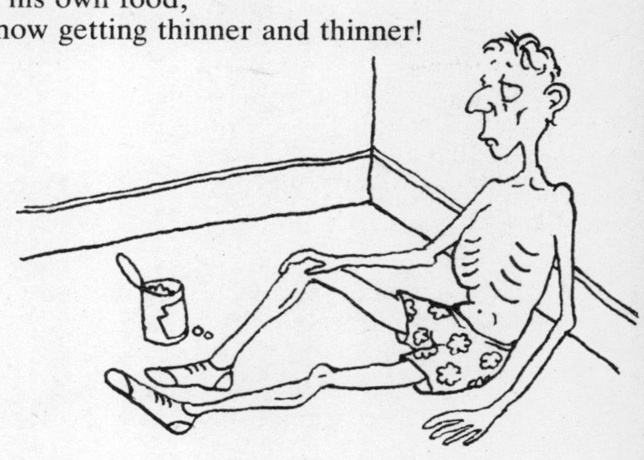

That's Entertainment

A soprano named Nancy McClee
Would sing, for quite a large fee.
Why people would pay
To hear her each day
Is a mystery – she sings so off key!

I have a piano that's grand,
With music propped up on its stand.
But I feel that a cello
Is really more mellow,
And I'd rather play that in a band.

The conductor of a band
Is perched on a little stand.
It's the musicians who play,
Yet he gets most pay –
Just for waving his hand!

There is a young girl in Shanghai
Who, as a soprano, sings high.
One day in the choir,
She sang even higher
When she sat on a pin and sprang high.

There once was a lady from Tring
Whose talent was that she could sing.
Her only desire
Was to sing in the choir,
And auditions are held in the spring.

An opera star in Vienna
Dyed her hair with henna;
But brown showed through
As she sang Act Two,
And ruined the pitch of the tenor.

There was a young lad named Mark
Who sang with the voice of a lark.
Then his throat got sore,
And his tones grew poor;
Now he sounds like a dog with a bark.

A production of *The Mikado*
Was presented in Colorado,
With stars Doris Day
And Faye Dunaway,
Who both sang with great bravado.

There was a man from Hong Kong
Who wrote a popular song:
'Nothing could be finer
Than to be in old Red China',
Which he played on piano and gong.

Young boys who play on flutes
Are rarely hairy brutes;
But one fine day,
Their sweet voices may
Deepen right down to their boots.

There was a flautist called Phil
Who, refusing to play even one trill,
Said: 'I'll continue to play
When someone will pay
At least a part of my bill.'

Is it true that Robinson Crusoe
In time on his island grew so
Lonely and glum
That he started to hum,
And finally sang like Caruso.

A lady musician called Anna
Took a working trip to Havana.
She played on the tuba
For folks down in Cuba,
And dressed in a tropical manna.

An orchestral conductor called Priddle,
Observed to a cellist in the middle,
'You have twixt your thighs,
My boy, a great prize –
With which you just sit and fiddle.'

There was an old man called Silas,
Who often tried to beguile us
By singing a song;
But the notes were all wrong,
So he only managed to rile us.

A trumpeter known as Chas
Formed a small band which has
Musicians who swing;
They each play and sing
Modern and Dixieland jazz.

A poor musician called Nina
Wanted a concertina.
But she could play a rag
On the top of the bag
Of her mother's old vacuum cleaner.

There was a young lady of Onga,
Who 'specially liked dancing the conga.
It's really divine –
You dance in a line,
Which quickly gets longa and longa.

A man who was learning bassoon
Could hardly play it in tune.
When he got a note right,
He'd play it all night,
And through to the afternoon.

A patriotic musician called Dawn
Was asked to play the French horn.
She said, 'Oh no,
I must play oboe;
And besides, I'm English born.'

A lady whose last name was Hester,
Danced often with Victor Sylvester.
Their steps would go
From quick-quick to slow,
At ballrooms in Leicester and Chester.

There was a young lady so proud,
Who started to sing very loud.
When people heard her,
They said they preferred her
To sing far away on a cloud.

A charming young singer named Hannah
Got caught in a flood in Savannah;
As she floated away,
Her sister, they say,
Accompanied her on the piannah!

The young man, Zachariah,
Said he could sing – the liar!
Not one true note
Came from his throat,
So we threw him out of the choir.

An angel who sat on a cloud
Was only one of a crowd.
They all played harps
With flats and sharps –
The neighbours complained, 'Too loud!'

A musical student called Carter,
Was a truly magnificent farter;
On the strength of a bean
He'd fart 'God Save The Queen',
And Beethoven's *Moonlight Sonata*.

When a disco-dancer had the notion
To set his hips in whirling motion,
He found he was able
To knock over a table,
Which caused uncommon commotion.

There is a young boy called Edgar
Who's learning to strum a guitar.
He practises long
To learn a new song,
But knows just the first verse so far.

I once knew a comic called Dawn,
Whose jokes were as ripe as old corn.
She'd try to be punny,
But just wasn't funny.
I wished that she'd never been born.

I knew a girl named Monica;
She lives in Greece, in Salonika.
In the dark of the night
With the stars shining bright,
She skilfully plays the harmonica.

A young musician looked glum,
He said to his dad and mum,
'I have a chance
To play at a dance,
But I can't find the sticks for my drum!'

There once was a young girl named Margo,
Who married a man from Chicago.
They played a duet
On an old spinet –
A piece from a Mendelsohn largo.

An astronaut called Dan Boone
In space began to croon.
His voice was flat –
Because of that
They left him on the moon!

I know of a dancer called Jake
Who likes to wiggle and shake.
His body churns,
Twists and turns,
And he moves just like a snake.

Ouch!

Where does it hurt?

An unfortunate man called Zebedee,
Was involved in a fight of some gravity.
When hit on the chin
His eyeballs fell in –
Now he can't even look for a remedy.

A horse-rider started to bound
Where forests and woods abound.
He drove his poor horse
Through a big bush of gorse,
And ended up flat on the ground.

Paul Smith-Minor

A very old man named Paul
Was watching a game of football.
He tried to partake,
Which was a mistake –
Paul stumbled and had a hard fall.

Smith-Minor, whose first name was Paul,
Just narrowly missed a bad fall.
He broke several teeth
And the jaw-bone beneath,
Several ribs, and a leg – but that's all.

An elegant man from Soho
Had a very bad fall in the snow-ho.
With his dignity shaken
More care now he's takin' –
He's careful, but terribly slow-ho!

All the boys from the Isle of Wight
Made great fun of Ermintrude Wright.
But their bottoms were sore
When they fell to the floor –
They didn't know that she could fight.

There was an old man of Blackheath
Who sat on his set of false teeth.
Said he, with a start,
'O Lord, bless my heart!
I haf biffen meshelf underneath.'

A dozy young lady named Gert
Was quite understandably hurt
When hit by some sticks
And a barrage of bricks;
She really must be more alert!

There was a young woman called Grace,
Who entered a fast steeplechase.
But her horse grew quite tense,
As it approached the first fence,
And poor Grace landed flat on her face.

There was an old tramp called May
Who slept in a load of soft hay.
She let out a squawk
When a long sharp pitchfork
Was thrust through the hay where she lay.

A bear who eats only honey
(Preferring the thick to the runny),
Was stung by bees
On all four knees,
But he didn't find that funny!

A certain old man named Sam,
Went for a ride on a tram.
A thief asked for money;
Said Sam, 'That's not funny',
And punched him a wham and a bam.

A girl with both arms in a sling
Went for a ride on a swing.
She had little hope
Of holding the rope,
But still, she gave it a fling!

In the city of San Francisco
I dance at a fashionable disco.
The music blares out,
I twist and shout,
Oops – I've just slipped my disc – oh!

Sweet little Emily Rose
Was tired and sought some repose.
But her sister, named Clare,
Put a tack on her chair,
And sweet little Emily Rose!

There was a young man named Ed
Who didn't sleep well on his bed.
He slumbered much more
Lying flat on the floor –
Till somebody stomped on his head!

> A worker who started to doze,
> Received a strong punch on the nose.
> His nose turned bright red,
> Swelled up and then bled –
> The worker now knows not to doze.

Quicksands burp and bubble,
Better cross them at the double;
If not, you see,
You soon will be
Up to your neck in trouble.

> I know a fellow named Beale,
> Who thinks he's not really real.
> When I pinch him he cries:
> 'That hurts!' – then he sighs,
> 'I guess if I feel then I'm real.'

At Christmas we visit Aunt Molly
Who's usually funny and jolly;
But last Boxing day,
Her temper gave way
When she fell in a load of green holly.

> There is a big girl called Brenda –
> You'd be wise not to offend her.
> For she gave a slap
> To one saucy chap
> Who offered to mend her suspender.

A Welshman named Llewellyn
Dug a dungeon to dwell in;
But forgot to build stairs,
And arrived unawares
In his cell – poor Llewellyn fell in.

> An Indian chief at a talk
> Let out a hell of a squawk.
> The sound was quite throaty,
> Just like a cayote –
> He'd sat on a sharp tomahawk!

A wise old prophet in Burma
Was frequently heard to murmur,
'Don't walk your dog
In marsh or on bog –
Go out where the ground is much firmer.'

> An unfortunate man, Stanley Hope,
> Started to ski down a slope.
> The slant was steep;
> The snow was deep;
> Did Stanley make it? Nope!

On a hot summer's day on his bicycle,
Lenny peddles whilst eating an icicle;
If he loses his grip,
He'll start to slip,
And he'll wish that he still had his tricycle.

A WISE OLD PROPHET IN BURMA...

I was bad at speaking and gramma,
So I took up throwing the hamma.
I hit my own head
And now I'm in bed,
And I can't even stutter or stamma.

> I have an Auntie Mo
> Who's really quite whacko.
> She took a gun
> To shoot her son,
> But missed, and hit her toe.

A swimmer in the Adriatic
Was floating about quite static.
But when he saw
A fin and a jaw,
His movements became quite dramatic!

> There was a young boy called Jim
> Who fractured his right lower limb.
> He leapt in a pool
> Without water – the fool.
> Good heavens, he must have been dim!

A big-bottomed swimmer from Sark
Dived into the sea after dark.
When a shark took a lump
From his rather large rump,
He gained a strange water-mark!

> An adventurous woman called Sue
> Was looking to do something new.
> She learned how to box,
> But took some hard knocks,
> And her face now is all black and blue.

A certain Miss Margaret Brown
Was awarded the May Queen crown.
But it's very great weight,
I'm sad to relate,
Caused Margaret Brown to frown.

> My friend, who comes from Stanmore,
> Fell asleep by the seashore.
> Her eyebrows were fried,
> She was burnt on each side,
> And her cheeks were painfully sore.

A lad in a blue sailor-suit
Looked sweet, but he was a brute.
He went to a show,
And what do you know,
He pelted the singer with fruit!

> A foolish, young girl named Kate
> Sat down on a farmer's gate.
> A bull, in despair,
> Tossed her high in the air,
> And she didn't come down until eight!

Mickey Mouse was in his house,
Taking off his trousers;
Then his mum
Smacked his bum
And chased him round the houses.

There was an old man from Penzance,
Who always wore sheet-iron pants;
He said, 'Some years back,
I sat on a tack,
And I'll never again take a chance!'

A hard-hearted boy called Neil
Claimed he didn't know how to feel.
But when I put some ants
Down the seat of his pants,
That boy certainly let out a squeal.

There was a young man called Spencer
Who really could not have been denser.
He was totally thick
And he started to pick
A fight with a champion fencer!

There was an old man from Dunoon
Who set out on a trip by balloon.
The man came off worst
When the big balloon burst,
And he landed back home rather soon.

Beware

There was a young man by the Nile
Who decided he'd swim for a while –
But why did he pause?
He saw the great jaws
Of a perfectly huge crocodile.

A boy on a bike with no light
Put out his hand to turn right.
He should have been fined
(In fact that's too kind),
Because this happened at night!

You mustn't try to grab
A very bad-tempered crab.
For if you do,
I'm telling you,
Its pincers will give you a jab.

There was a young man named Jake,
Who ate some heavy, sweet cake
Before a swim
(Hard luck on him) –
They're having to drag the lake.

Insulting behaviour

Said a very outspoken lass,
Who liked to abuse and harass:
'My dear, your ears
Have been growing for years,
And you're getting to look like an ass.'

A youngish man called Daniel
Was rude to old Nathaniel;
He said: 'Your nose
Is red, like a rose,
And your ears hang down, like a spaniel!'

    A sensitive lady of Chelsea
    Spent a weekend at Selsey.
    When asked if alone,
    She said, 'Mind your own,
    I'm just not going to tell, see!'

A batsman who was on the large side,
Was heckled by an opponent who cried:
'When he's at the wicket
It's not really cricket;
Is that what's meant by a wide?'

Relative Values

My father was a sad man,
My brother was a bad man;
My sister and mother
Just hated each other:
No wonder I'm such a madman!

My mum has reached the stage
Of getting into a rage
With crumpled shirts,
And socks and skirts,
For it's not the Iron Age.

    There once was a small boy called Joe Joe,
    Who wanted a red and blue yo-yo.
    Poor Joe Joe grew sad
    When his mum and his dad
    Said, 'Right now a yo-yo's a no no.'

I have a very nice Dadda,
But never has he been madder;
While mending a roof-tile,
He noticed my big smile,
As I sauntered away with his ladder.

I know a helpful laddie
Who has a golfing daddy.
In gorse he crawls
To find lost balls,
'Cause daddy has no caddy.

    'Dear Mother,' wrote wee Jimmy Broon,
    'I've dug a hole twenty feet doon.
    I'll ignore my aching back,
    Till I strike oil that is black.'
    So she sent him a card, 'Get well soon!'

    In skool exams, I'm exceling,
    So I rote my muther forteling
    All the results mite
    Be kwite all rite;
    Well, except perhaps for my speling!

    I had a very strict dad,
    Who hit me each time he was mad.
    But I hit him back,
    Whack after whack –
    Now he calls me a strapping young lad!

I told a joke to my pa.
He listened and went: 'Ha, ha,
Ha ha, ha ha,
Ha ha, ha ha,
Ha ha...ven't you anything better to do than waste your
   time telling jokes that aren't even funny?'

There was an old man from Nantucket,
Who kept all his cash in a bucket.
His daughter, named Nan,
Ran away with a man,
And as for the bucket, Nan-tuck-et.

The warnings from my mother,
Or even from my brother,
Cause me no fear:
They're in one ear,
And simply out the other.

A baby in the cot
Smoked and drank a lot.
I blame the mum
Who gave him rum –
Such a dear little tot!

It used to be a jolly hour,
Putting up the holly bough;
But Christmas last
We were aghast
When Dad, instead, used cauliflower.

There was an old maid of Lincoln,
Who made a considerable stink on
The subject of furs –
For a young neice of hers
Had run off with nothing but mink on!

There was a young man called Bill
Who used an electric drill.
It's all rather boring,
And father kept roaring:
'That noise is making me ill.'

I have a constructive daughter,
So for her birthday I bought her
A book that tells all
About building a wall,
With plenty of sweat, bricks and mortar.

There was an old lady of Seaton,
Who asked for a chair, once she'd eaten.
When told by her son
'You're sitting on one,'
Said she, 'It's to put up my feet on.'

A surly Scottish laddie
Had an Irish daddy:
He said, 'I'm not
A proper Scot –
I'm living with a Paddy.'

A movie actor's my daddy.
He often tells me, 'Laddie –
I never survive
A western alive.
Why am I always the baddie?'

A grandmother who couldn't be sterner,
Grabbed her granddaughter and threatened to burn her.
But the girl seized the cat
And said, 'Granny, burn that!'
For at cruelty that girl was a learner.

There was a young man from Calcutta
Who constantly ate peanut butter.
His mother would say
To his father each day,
'I'm sure that our son is a nutter!'

I've got a hooligan daughter,
I expect the police may have caught 'er.
She said as she threw
A bottle or two,
'I'm a typical football supporter.'

A family's up at dawning,
Moaning, stretching and yawning.
They get out of bed,
And oh how they dread
Going to work in the morning.

The kid next door's a punk
His room's all cluttered with junk.
His mother saw
The mess on the floor
And screamed, 'Pack it all in a trunk.'

I knew a girl named Florence
Who held in great abhorrence
The work she did
For Uncle Sid,
As well as Uncle Lawrence.

Tastes Peculiar

There was a young lady of Strood
Who was mighty fussy with food.
The meat she would eat
(An occasional treat)
Had to be carefully stewed.

A millionaire's son went on trips
In jets and luxury ships;
But all he would eat,
In cold or in heat,
Were platefuls of burgers and chips.

A man named Ali MacBasta
Would only eat heaps of egg pasta.
For breakfast and lunch
On pasta he'd munch,
Gulping it faster and faster.

My brother likes to munch
Carrots for his lunch.
They can't be beat –
That's all he'll eat;
He buys them by the bunch.

There once was a young man who'd feast
On nothing but lumps of fresh yeast.
It was hard in the morn
To rise up at dawn,
But the yeast got him started as least.

There was a young lady of Ash
Who always ate sausage and mash.
She found that sweet jelly
Would fatten her belly,
And make her break out in a rash!

There was a young man called Sam,
Who was so fond of strawberry jam
That he'd not only spread
Two inches on bread,
But also on chicken and lamb!

There was a young lady from Slough,
Who drank her milk straight from the cow.
To her udder delight
She could drink through the night:
Amazing, but don't ask me how!

A vegetarian called Pam
Wouldn't eat pork or ham.
Well to tell you the truth,
She had a sweet tooth
And all that she *would* eat was jam.

There was a young cannibal, Joe,
Who used to eat plates of cod's roe.
His mother said, 'Sonny,
It's not very funny;
You ought to eat people you know!'

There once was a fellow called Ted
Who liked to drink soup while in bed.
But one day it spilt
All over his quilt,
So he ate all his bedclothes instead.

A struggling artist who lived in a garret
Had two gold rings of 24-carat.
One day in despair,
He cooked the pair
To feed himself and his parrot.

A man who loved to eat custard,
One day got hot and flustered,
For he dipped in his spoon
And discovered quite soon
That the stuff he was eating was mustard.

There is a young man of Yalding
Who likes to drink tea when it's scalding.
The result of the heat
Is pigeon-toed feet,
And a head that is rapidly balding!

There was an old lady of Norwich,
Whose diet was high in roughage.
She was terribly keen
On the common baked bean,
And she got the wind up with porridge.

A fish is soon going to dine
On a worm that's hooked on a line.
The poor worm is turning,
It's wiggling and squirming.
To the fish it will taste just divine.

There was an old lady called Pru
Who dropped her false teeth in the stew.
Said a sensitive waiter,
'It's horrid to cater
For careless old females like you.'

'Waiter! This soup has a smell
Reminiscent of brimstone from hell.
The taste is as foul
As a decomposed owl,
And it looks like the slime on a well.'

There was a girl of New York
Who liked to eat pies of pork.
Sometimes at lunch
On six she would munch,
And still find time to talk.

A girl on a train in Florida
Couldn't have been any horrider.
She ate fish and chips,
And spat orange pips
All along the corridor!

There was a cook from Cork
Who gave a TV talk
On Irish stew,
So thick that you
Had to eat it with a garden fork.

Vinegar's made from malt,
I love it to a fault.
I soak my chips,
And lick the drips,
And cover the lot in salt.

There was a young lady who said,
'Now remember I want a good spread,
With puppy dogs' tails,
And brown roasted snails,'
But she ended up sick in her bed.

There was an old lady of Crewe
Who made a thick, tasty stew
From toads and frogs
She found in bogs.
But she just couldn't eat it – could you?

A hungry young woman called Trish
Was given a plateful of fish.
The matter was putrid
Omitting foul liquid,
So she dumped it and just ate the dish.

There was a young man who loved Brie –
Years old and extremely runny.
It gave off a pong
So exceedingly strong –
To eat it was pure bravery.

My greedy sister Nelly can
Make you believe she's a pelican.
It's not absurd,
For just like that bird,
Her beak can hold more than her belly can!

We bought cream cakes and a bun
For a picnic out in the sun.
She drank cups of tea
From twelve until three,
And never offered me one!

A sloppy young man likes to eat
Desserts that are gooey and sweet.
He consumes jelly and cream
With manners obscene,
And licks what he spills on his feet.

A foul-mannered man, Mr Bustard,
Liked to sweeten his tea with custard.
His conduct was gross,
He'd lick jam off his toast,
And his guests were truly disgusted.

Do you really, Nelly, wish
To eat from that round dish?
It only contains
Unpleasant remains
Of jelly and old smelly fish.

There was a young lady of Cork
Whose favourite meal was pork.
She picks at her meat
(It's not very neat),
But she never will use knife or fork.

A baby sat in a pram
Eating a leg of lamb.
His distraught mother said,
'We found that his bed
Was covered with joints of roast ham.'

There was a young man called Dale
Who wanted to eat a whale.
He mashed it with cheese,
And served it with peas,
But couldn't quite manage the tail.

I eat peas with honey,
I've done it all my life.
They do taste kind of funny –
But it keeps them on the knife!

Eccentrics

There was a strange fellow called Matt,
Who was dressed up to look like a cat.
His feet were like paws,
With retractable claws,
And whiskers grew out from his hat.

There once was a daring park warden
Who thought, as he lay in his garden,
'If caught in this nudeness,
I think there's no rudeness,
So long as I mutter, "Beg pardon!" '

An eccentric old person of Slough,
Took all his meals with a cow,
Saying, 'Though my memory is hazy,
I think mother was like Daisy.'
But he never would indicate how.

A famous surgeon, it's been said,
Stored mutilated limbs under his bed.
They later found there
The leg of a chair,
A book-spine and a broom's head.

There was an old man of Thermopylae,
Renowned for his inordinate sloppery;
They said, 'If you choose
To boil eggs in your shoes,
You're egg yolks will never cook properly.'

There was a young man called Vince,
Who made a poor barber wince:
He used the leg of his chair
To comb through his hair,
Then demanded to have a pink rinse!

Said a simple young girl called Sue,
'There's something in my shoe.'
But what do you know,
It was only her toe,
So she stuck it back on with strong glue.

There once was a young man of Keïstick,
Who always ate soup with a chop-stick;
For he said, 'As I eat
Neither fish, fowl nor meat,
I would not want to finish too quick.'

There was a young lady of Slough,
Who claimed she didn't know how
To quack like a duck,
Though she tried without luck –
But boy, she sure could meow.

There was a young man from Quebec
Who wrapped both his legs round his neck.
But then he forgot
How to undo the knot,
And now he's an absolute wreck!

AN ECCENTRIC OLD PERSON OF SLOUGH...

A timid young man when a tot
Fell into a giant teapot.
But as he grew older,
That man grew bolder,
And flew out of the spout like a shot.

> There was a young girl named Anna
> Who had a superior manner.
> She drove fast cars
> To cocktail bars,
> And puffed on a mammoth Havana.

I once knew a very bald chap
Who put his head under a tap
To wash all his hair,
Which just wasn't there –
So he'd not remove his cap.

> An Irishwoman called Rosalie
> Would use a broom if paid a fee.
> She'd start before dawn
> In the mountains of Mourne.
> And sweep right down to the sea.

A businessman called Signor Prado
Tried to buy Colorado.
Some doctors from Spain
Examined his brain,
And discovered it filled with bravado!

> There was an old man of Neath,
> Who drilled holes in all of his teeth.
> When he drank water
> He'd squirt his young daughter,
> 'Cause water would spurt through his teeth.

There was a young model called Lola
Dressed in a black suit and bowler.
With briefcase and brolly,
She looked simply jolly,
Skating to work on one roller.

> One day my Aunty Milly
> Walked to Piccadilly.
> 'I can't tell you why,'
> She said with a sigh,
> 'I must have been awfully silly!'

There was a lady named Nelly
Who mucked out the pigs in one welly.
When asked by her mother,
Would she please wear the other,
She said, 'But it's really too smelly.'

> A Swiss man resembling a beaver
> Lived under the lake in Geneva,
> He swam and he swam,
> And installed by the dam
> A sub-aqua TV receiver.

A very old man called Jonah,
At the market in Barcelona,
Put up for sale
A giant grey whale;
Said he, 'It needs a new owner.'

A certain young lady called Lily
Likes knickers – light pink and frilly.
In winter she wears
Maybe three or four pairs,
To keep her from feeling too chilly.

An eccentric old man called Bill
Lived in a cottage in Dill.
He dried his socks
On the window-box,
And his underwear on the sill!

There was an old man from Whitehaven,
Whose whiskers had never been shaven;
He said, 'It is best,
For they make a nice nest,
In which I can keep my pet raven!'

There once was a kind-hearted king
Who taught a poor chicken to sing
By using his crown
To bang, 'till sundown,
On a kettle tied up with a string.

Occupational Hazards

A young man who had chosen
To go to sea as a bosun
Is in a poor way,
Just north of Norway,
With all of his assets frozen!

There is an old man in York
Who draws on the pavement with chalk.
He makes a few pence,
But he gets very tense
When over his work people walk!

There was a young gardener from Leeds,
Who swallowed a packet of seeds.
In less than an hour
His nose was a flower
And his head was a bunch of weeds.

A sailor in the Atlantic
Suddenly became quite frantic.
He shook with great fear
When his ship sailed too near
An iceberg that was gigantic.

A policeman pounding a beat
Can never rest on a seat.
They must persevere,
And keep walking I fear –
Even with two aching feet.

There was a Welsh dentist called Keith,
Whose practice was well-known in Neath.
Perfecting his skill,
He made himself ill,
Extracting all of his teeth.

There was an old florist call Bower
Who took a very cold shower.
He watered his skin
From his toes to his chin,
And out of his nose grew a flower.

Farmers' boys have to learn
That chickens can be quite stern.
If you grab their eggs
From between their legs,
They'll bite your bum in return.

There was a young sailor from China,
Who cruised on an ocean liner.
He lost his pigtail
In a violent gale,
Just off Asia Minor.

I know of a man who's a Quaker,
He works dawn to dusk as a baker.
But one day by mistake
He was cooked with a cake,
And now he is meeting *his* Maker!

Committee members at Shoreham
Find that the chairman bores 'em;
A few are bleating,
'There's never a meeting
Because we can't get a full quorum.'

The Fireman's Lament

The firemen were having tea –
It must have been half past three.
But then came a call,
And out they rushed all,
To save a cat up a tree.

How many cats can there be
At any one time up a tree?
The fire brigade came
And said, 'What a game!'
Then rescued all twenty-three!

'If the cat's trapped up a tree
Don't send again for me,'
The fireman said
(His name was Ned),
'I've missed my lunch and tea!'

Animal Antics

You know that a pig is a hog
And can tell a cat from a dog;
But it's perfectly true
That all of them do
Look very alike in thick fog.

    We all know that furry white rabbits
    Breed quickly – it's one of their habits.
    They canoodle all day,
    Hop, skip and play –
    That's life for Nature's own rabbits.

There is a cat in Wales,
Whose patience often fails.
He smashes the dishes
When he angrily swishes
Each one of his nine long tails.

    Meet Miss Piggy Piggle
    Watch her give a wiggle.
    Her beau is Sam,
    He's quite a ham,
    And both will make you giggle.

There once were two cats of Kilmany,
Each thought there was one cat too many.
So they quarrelled and fit,
They scratched and they bit,
Till instead of two cats, there weren't any.

    At dawn the bees from a hive
    Looked round for pollen to thrive,
    In one London park garden
    Were told: 'Beg your pardon;
    This park is not open 'till five.'

When an ass and a mare one day
Said to their son, 'By the way,
You do know that you'll
Grow up as a mule.'
He started to bray, 'Neigh, neigh.'

    A jackdaw had clipped to its wing
    A beautiful golden ring
    'It's eighteen carat,'
    Explained a green parrot,
    'It's valuable; quick, pawn the thing.'

There was a dog, a Great Dane,
Who hadn't got much of a brain.
He'd chase a hare,
That just wasn't there,
And he'd do it again and again.

    A cat in the town of St. Ives
    Stole honey from several large hives.
    Once stung by eight bees,
    He said: 'Stop it please!
    You know I have only nine lives.'

There once was a lazy, green frog
Who rode on the back of a dog.
But the dog wasn't big,
So he moved to a pig:
You could say he's gone the whole hog!

There once was an elegant fox,
Who was given a pair of striped socks;
But to cover each paw,
He needed to have four –
So he hopped to the shop for more stocks.

There was a small mouse from Cheam,
Whose whiskers were covered in cream.
What a to-do,
That stuff sticks like glue,
And it had to be boiled off with steam.

There once was a cat called Tat,
Who grew most incredibly fat.
He sat on the floor
And ate more and more,
Till . . . pop! . . . that was the end of Tat.

Pets' corner

A dog I used to own,
Would never touch a bone.
He'd only eat
The finest meat,
And he'd order it by phone!

My tortoise, Araminta,
Is really not a sprinter;
She does the crawl
From spring to fall,
Then sleeps all through the winter.

There was a young girl called Molly,
Whose favourite pet was a collie.
When she went for a jog,
This highly-trained dog
Would strut right behind with her brolly!

We have an intelligent cat,
Who refuses to hunt mouse or rat.
She'll lie still and wait
For food on her plate;
Now who can blame her for that?

There once was a girl named Ida
Who made a pet of a spider.
This thoughtful befriending
Had a sad ending –
The spider drank all of her cider!

The cat who ate up my curry,
I threw in a lake down in Surrey;
Instead of expirin',
He came home enquirin':
'Any more curry? Please hurry.'

I own a brown hunting doggy
Who loves to chase when its foggy.
His instincts and habits
Direct him to rabbits –
And sometimes a scraggy old moggy.

I have a pet, an armadillo,
Which I found beneath a willow.
I took it to bed
To rest my head,
But it makes an uncomfortable pillow.

My cat's got up a tree –
Most bothersome to me.
Now, pussy come down
Or I'll break your crown,
And toss you into the sea.

That dog of Aunty Meg's
Often sits up and begs:
He'll get a cuppa,
To follow his suppa
Of bacon and scrambled eggs.

I once owned a little green turtle,
A slow pet whose first name was Myrtle.
She had babies galore –
Then kept having more!
That turtle was certainly fertile.

Our dog, a Labrador,
Occupies half of the floor.
He's getting so fat
He covers his mat,
Most of the carpet and more!

There once was a man with two poodles,
Whose names were Toodles and Doodles.
Their favourite dish
Was not meat or fish;
The poodles loved oodles of noodles!

Our dog has a cosy box
All lined with cushions and socks.
But he can't eat there,
In his private lair,
Its too sticky from toffee and chocs.

There was a girl called Amanda
Who owned a bear – a panda.
They both sipped tea
From twelve till three
On Amanda's large veranda.

A woman in Amsterdam
Is often seen wheeling a pram.
Look close and see,
How surprised you will be –
In the pram is a real baby lamb!

There once was a woman called Kookoo,
Who owned a real Swiss cuckoo.
Each hour was heard
A sound from that bird –
That cuckoo drove poor Kookoo cuckoo!

Wild animals

There was female antelope
Who loved a big male antelope.
But he banged his knee
Against an oak tree,
And so now they can't elope.

There once was a jolly fat hippo
Who jumped in the sea for a dippo.
It would have been wise
Had he opened his eyes,
But he didn't and flattened a ship – oh!

I know a grizzly bear
Who has a comfy lair.
It's really snug
With a lovely rug
And one enormous chair.

Do you wish to ride on a camel?
There's one here that's known as Gamel.
I warn you, don't try,
He'll spit in your eye –
He's a most peculiar mammal.

A wild, buoyant beast is the dingo,
Who'll howl and dance the flamingo,
Before he trots off
On the lead of a toff,
To watch his rich master play bingo.

National bird of the USA,
The eagle, seen at the dawn of day.
It soars in flight
With a head that's white,
This bird is bald and needs a toupee!

Zoo capers

A girl who observed a gorilla
Discovered the beast could thrill 'er.
He rattled his cage
In a furious rage,
Then swallowed a small caterpillar!

A girl who used to shake
At the sight of a baby snake,
Went to the zoo
And came home with two –
She feeds them on home-made cake.

In the zoo there's an animal, Hamel –
A spitting, young, ornary camel.
He'd rather be free,
Like a bird or a bee,
And hates being classified 'Mammal'.

My mother passed out at the zoo
When she saw the baboons in full view.
I ran to the keeper,
And told him to keep 'er
Until she awoke and came to.

Though big, a hippopotamus
Is very clearly not a bus,
Although at the zoo,
For a quid or two,
He gave a fun ride to the lot of us.

A chimp from Ballawong
Sat the whole day long,
Beating his chest
Without any rest,
Declaring: 'I'm really King Kong!'

Said a tiger at the zoo,
Talking with a kangaroo,
'With all this hot dust,
I think that I must
Give myself a shampoo.'

A jungle's a wond'rous place,
More wild than out in space.
The lion may eat
Fresh-slaughtered meat,
But first he'll kneel down and say grace.

An elephant born in Tibet,
One day in its cage wouldn't get.
So its keeper stood near,
Stuck a hose in its ear,
And invented the first Jumbo Jet.

There was a young girl called Amba
Who charmed a snake – a mamba.
With a hypnotic glance,
She made the snake dance
To a rhumba, tango and samba.

The gull is called a kittiwake,
And people near the shore awake
To feed this bird,
When winds are heard,
With bread and bits of gritty cake.

There was a young man at the zoo
Who heard an enormous 'Moo'.
He thought, 'That's not a sow,
But it could be a cow . . .'
In fact, it was a large caribou!

I went to the zoo with Bruce.
We both drank a bottle of juice.
I fed some whelks
To a herd of elks,
And Bruce put his head in a moose!

There once was a bald gorilla
Who, wrapped up in a furry chinchilla,
Escaped from a zoo
Through a gap in the loo,
And now works in a cafe in Manilla.

Farm frolics

The sound that cows make is mooo,
That's what they usually dooo;
Except when grass grows
Way up to their nose –
Then they will sneeze, 'Achooo!'

Can you tell me how
A top-class dairy cow
(A winner, you know,
At a country show)
Can curtsey or take a bow?

There was a young lady called Gwen,
Who started wondering when
She would ever see
An egg for her tea –
But was her chicken a hen?

A certain young lady of Slough
Is widely considered a cow.
Her name is Mary –
She's down at the dairy,
Along with the hen and the sow.

A woman named Harriet Teacher
Thought the hen a most elegant creature.
When the hen heard of that,
She laid eggs in her hat,
Rewarding kind Harriet Teacher.

One day a poor nervous goose
Was frightened to death by a moose:
It stood on one leg
And laid a big egg;
Then all of its feathers came loose.

A farmer from Looe
Bought a cow, named Sue.
He taught her to speak
In English and Greek,
But all she could say was *Moo*!

A farmer with hens in his yard
Decided to watch them, on guard.
But one angry fox
Threw many large rocks,
Which, really, the farmer found hard.

Curiouser and curiouser

A curious bird is the bunting,
You'll hear it if you go hunting.
It has an odd cry
That sounds like a sigh,
And a railway engine shunting.

A curious bird is the crow,
The blackest fowl I know.
It's out of sight
In the middle of the night –
But how does it hide in the snow?

A curious bird is the gull,
Which lives on the isle of Mull.
Just on a hunch,
It flew out to lunch
On some fish in nearby Hull.

There once lived a bird, the Great Auk,
Who was unable to walk or to talk.
Although it would try,
It just couldn't fly
And it only let out a big squawk.

A wonderful bird is the Toucan,
It eats just as much as you can.
Is it able to speak
With food in its beak?
It's said that the one at the zoo can.

A beautiful bird is the jay
With plumage exceedingly gay.
It chunters and chatters
On various matters,
Whilst flying along on its way.

A wonderful bird is the sparrow,
It flies as straight as an arrow.
It sometimes sings,
And folds its wings
And goes to sleep in a barrow.

A curious bird is the linnet;
It won't stop singing for a minute.
With its voice so sweet,
It should try to compete
For a musical prize – it might win it!

There stood a very big ostrich,
Who was naked, not wearing a stitch.
When I asked him why,
He claimed with a sigh,
'I'm just a poor bird, not rich.'

A very odd insect, the gnat,
It never stops for a chat.
But it loves to bite,
Both day and night,
And uses its mouth for that!

A curious insect, the centipede,
When racing is always in the lead.
It'll win its heat
By a hundred feet –
How on earth does it crawl with such speed?

A Chinese dog is a chow
(An oriental bow-wow),
Which growls at cats
On Persian mats,
But respects the holy cow.

Remember that dog, the chow,
The oriental bow-wow.
It's been known
To answer the phone
Saying 'Moo', just like a cow!

A strange little beast is the hare,
Even to see it is rare.
It has the habit,
Just like the white rabbit,
Of suddenly not being there!

A mischievous beast is the goat;
It seldom rides in a boat.
Although on land
I understand
Its smell is worthy of note!

An unfunny beast is the jackal,
Which seems, indeed, to lack all
Sense of humour;
Well, that's the rumour,
For it's never been known to cackle.

An unusual beast is the Kinkajou;
Its fur is like mink to me and you.
If seen in a club,
Or even a pub,
It's likely to down a stiff drink or two.

A curious beast is the monkey.
It may be thin or chunky.
If it has green hair,
And rings on its ears,
It must be a punky monkey.

A most unusual carp
Works hard at playing the harp.
But whenever he tries
The poor fish cries,
For each note he plays is quite sharp.

A curious fish is the chub,
Framed on the wall of a pub.
It took some bait
It shouldn't have ate,
And got hooked on the wrong sort of grub!

A CURIOUS BEAST IS THE MONKEY...

A very strange fish is the conger;
It hardly could be any longer.
And if you coil it,
Then slowly boil it,
The smell will get stronger and stronger.

A curious fish is the hake.
It cannot live in a lake;
It needs the sea
To feel quite free,
And it's meat makes tasty fish cake.

A sensible fish is the brill,
He sleeps where waters are still.
And when there's a storm
He'll try to keep warm
By the wheel of an old water-mill.

Optimistically Speaking

It could always be worse

An optimistic young man called Ted,
Was born with a hole in his head.
'Good job it's not two,
Or the wind blowing through
Would make it draughty,' he said.

A very keen hiker called Pete
Ate pepper with his sweet.
Till one day, 'tis said
He sneezed off his head –
He's lucky it wasn't his feet.

A girl from Cardiff called Gwen
Stood at the foot of Big Ben.
At one o'clock
The clang was a shock;
Said she, 'I'm glad it's not ten!'

I know a guy called Claud,
Who had some trouble abroad.
He was bitten by bugs
And mugged by thugs:
Said he, 'Good thing I'm insured.'

I'm bored to death by Harrison;
His jokes and puns are embarrassin'.
But I quite like the bum.
He's as dumb as they come
Which makes me feel bright by comparison.

How to cope

A cheerful old bear at the zoo
Could always find something to do.
If it bored him to go
On a walk to and fro,
He'd turn round and walk fro and to.

In the dark dismal days of December
It is always a joy to remember
That come Christmas day,
You'll have on display
A turkey trussed up to dismember.

Neil and his performing seal

An entertainer called Neil
Trained a performing seal
To balance a rose
On the tip of its nose,
Whilst riding a bike with one wheel.

An amateur showman in Deal
Found the audience didn't show zeal.
So off he soon went
To elsewhere in Kent,
With his seal on a bike with one wheel.

There was a young lady of Leeds
Who planted an assortment of seeds.
The birds pecked up most,
But still she can boast
Of a rose in a garden of weeds.

A girl in the utmost alarm
Had a basket of eggs on her arm.
She tripped on her legs,
And they had scrambled eggs
For the next few days on the farm.

Keeping your cool

In situations of stress 'tis said,
This man can keep his head.
When a bird called a snipe
· Flew away with his pipe,
He lit a cigar instead.

A certain young goalie called Alvin,
Four goals in succession he let in.
When the captain cried,
He coolly replied,
'Then we only need five goals to win.'

There was a young wife from Uganda,
Renowned for her coolness and candour.
When, during abuse,
Someone said, 'You goose!'
She quickly retorted, 'Uganda!'

There was a young lad called Murray
Who flatly refused to hurry.
He said to his mate,
'You'll just have to wait
As rushing about causes worry.'

A suicidal chum
Looked all down and glum:
'I'll take my life
With this sharp knife.'
Said I: 'Why not, ho-hum.'

A gentleman dining in Kew
Once found a dead mouse in his stew:
'Don't wave it about,'
Said the head-waiter, Stout,
'Or the others will ask for one too!'

Looking on the bright side

There was a young girl called Joni,
Who ate plates of boiled macaroni.
She got very fat,
But she didn't mind that,
'Cos she bounced when she fell off her pony.

There was an old lady of Wales,
Who lived upon oysters and snails.
She soon grew a shell;
She said, 'It's as well,
Now I'll never need coats or veils.'

There was a young man called Shane,
Who had a very small brain.
He wasn't too bright,
But that was all right,
'Cause headaches presented no pain.

Said the turkey to the bee,
'Christmas means the end of me.
You may be freezing
And miserably sneezing,
But at least I'll be roasting, see!'

Remember, don't be low
When your teeth fall out and go.
Just wait till the morning
And soon after dawning,
There'll be 10p under your pillow.

Enough to Make You Blush

There was a young man from Cheddar,
Whose face could not have been redder.
When he joked with George,
'Go jump in the gorge',
He did – and he couldn't be deader!

There once was a fellow called Hubert
Whose manners were most prim and pert.
When he saw a girl remove her sock,
He's never quite got over the shock –
He's just like a statue of stone, quite innert.

A certain young Scot called Bert
Is red-faced and terribly hurt.
For he stupidly spilt
Some tea on his kilt,
And is wearing his mother's plaid skirt.

I was swimming off Bermuda
When I met a barracuda.
Now where do you suppose
It put its big, wet nose?
Well, it couldn't have been ruder!

There was a young girl named Harris,
Whom doctors were wont to embarrass.
If one came to her bed
She'd blush a bright red –
Even in plaster of Paris!

Shocking, shocking, shocking,
A mouse ran up my stocking;
When it got to my knee,
Wow! What did it see?
Shocking, shocking, shocking!

I know a girl called Cher,
Who used to spit and swear
In language rare
(She didn't care) –
Her words would shock a bear!

There was a young man from Dumbarton,
Who thought he could run like a Spartan.
On the thirty-ninth lap
His braces went snap,
And his face went a red Scottish tartan.

There was a young sunbather from Bewes
Who lay on the bank of the Ouse.
His radio blared
And passers-by stared,
For all he had on was the news!

There was a girl from Swansea,
Who found that toilets aren't free.
When having no change,
She had to arrange,
To speedily borrow 2p!

There was a young man called John
Who didn't have very much on.
Said he, 'How the breeze
Tickles my knees;
Oh where have my warm trousers gone?'

A young belly-dancer from Hythe
Was extremely supple and lithe.
When a naughty spider
Crept somewhere insider 'er,
Oh did she wriggle and writhe.

There once was a ghost named Paul,
Who went to a fancy-dress ball.
To shock all the guests
He went quite undressed,
But the rest couldn't see him at all!

A naughty boy with the strangest shape
Thought it would be a jolly good jape
For the fancy-dress ball
To wear nothing at all –
And to go as a naked ape!

A pretty young girl called Jean
Jumped high on a trampoline.
The boys laughed in roars
At the sight of her drawers –
The first bloomers they'd ever seen.

A young lady called out with a frown
When surprised by some callers from town,
'In a minute or less
I'll slip on a dress,'
But she slipped on the stairs and came down

I once had a girl-friend, Amy,
Who really knew how to shame me.
In the lounge of the Ritz
She yelled, 'What hairy armpits.'
So I ditched her – can anyone blame me?

There was a young lady of Tottenham,
Her manners – she'd wholly forgotten 'em.
Whilst at tea at the Vicar's
She took off her knickers,
Explaining she felt much too hot in 'em.

There was an old man of the West
Who wore a long woollen vest.
When I said, 'It doesn't fit,'
He replied, 'No, not a bit;
But to remove it would cause my arrest.'

An excessive quantity of rum(bling)
Set an acrobat's tum(bling).
His noises abdominal
Where simply phenomenal –
But everyone thought it was mum(bling)!

A lady of limited means
Lives only on peas and baked beans.
She doesn't have furs,
Her clothes aren't hers –
Which all leads to embarrassing scenes.

THERE WAS A YOUNG LADY OF TOTTENHAM...

Love and Marriage

Attraction

There is a man called Dan
Who has a golden tan.
He spends lots of money
On girls he calls 'Honey' –
Dan's a real ladies' man.

> There lives a tall dark man,
> Who's known as dashing Dan.
> He looks so brill
> That women will
> Kiss him when they can.

A Scotsman said to Annabelle:
'I dinna ken why Hannah fell
In love with my kilt,
Right up to the hilt.
She says herself she canna tell.'

> There once was a strong man in Russia,
> Whose flat could not have been plusher.
> Girls came to his place,
> But found his embrace
> Was more like a giant car-crusher.

A handsome man named Bill,
Lives way up on the hill.
He's rough, he's mean,
And quite unclean,
Yet Doris loves him still.

> A certain young lady called Kate
> Stood up a boy on a date.
> She phoned up the guy,
> And he said with a sigh,
> 'You were more than normally late.'

A lovely young woman called Betty
Went for a walk on the jetty.
She met a tall seaman:
He's strong, such a he-man –
An officer who's said to be petty.

> There was a young girl named Dinah
> Who wanted to marry a miner.
> 'I'll tell you why –
> It's the gleam in his eye.'
> (But the lamp on his head is the shiner).

A very wise lady called Anne
Would have nothing to do with a man;
Until a pools winner
Took her out to dinner,
And flew with her off to Japan.

There was a young girl called Beryl
Who had a boy-friend named Cyril.
Her fond mother said,
'He's weak in the head –
If you marry him, it's at your peril!'

I know a boy at the Tech'
Who is a pain in the neck!
He just wants to kiss;
He claims that it's bliss –
So I let him give me a peck!

There is a girl called Lou,
She loves to bill and coo.
Give her a kiss
And the affectionate miss
Will promptly give you one too.

I know a young lad named John Morse,
Who's madly in love with a horse.
His best friend, Harry,
Asked if they'd marry,
To which he replied, 'Yes, of course!'

A girl I took out to dine
Said, 'Spaghetti is so divine.'
When we began our canoodles,
All of her long noodles
Got totally tangled with mine.

An ancient knight called Lancelot
Was known by all to glance a lot
At Queen Guinevere –
Even call her, 'My dear',
And take her out to dance a lot!

Unlucky in love

There was a young man named Big John,
Who fell deeply in love with a swan.
He now feels perplexed –
What to do next?
His darling's flown off; she has gone!

A silly, young lady named Ann
Went to a dance with a fan.
Though she kept herself cool,
That girl was a fool –
She could never be seen by a man.

A thoughtful young man called Clem
Picked a rose from a thorny stem.
He gave it to Alice
Who said, without malice,
'I'd rather have cash or a gem.'

There is an old spinster in Ryde,
Who has for many years tried
To get off the shelf,
And blames herself
For not yet being a bride.

There was a man called Neville
Who claimed he was on the level.
But when he kissed Sue,
He gave me one too –
That Neville is rather a devil.

A medieval girl named Emma
Had a close friend called Gemma;
But they started to fight
For they loved the same knight –
They were both in a common dilemma.

There was a young man called Barry,
Whose girl-friend refused to marry.
She said, 'It is sad
But I've got it quite bad;
You see, I'm just wild about Harry.'

A nautical man of Dundee
Devotedly wooed Miss Elly,
'Till one evening in summer-time
She said, 'Bill, it's maritime,'
And he immediately left for the sea.

There was a lad named Harry
Who fell in love with Carrie.
They both would sigh:
'One day we'll die
Committing Hari-Kari.'

She frowned and called him Mister,
Because in sport he kissed her;
And so in spite
That very night
This mister kissed her sister.

An innocent maiden of Gloucester
Fell in love with a young man named Foster:
She met him in Leicester,
But he merely carressed 'er –
Then that hard-hearted Foster just lost 'er.

My sister has a date
With a boy called Mortimer Chait.
She just can't wait
'Cos she thinks he's great;
But so far he's one week late!

A desperate girl called Jane,
Wanted a man on a chain.
She started to bargain
In old Copenhagen,
And now she has a great Dane!

Courting

There is a young boy called Larry,
Who lives right next door to Carrie.
Each child is four,
And what is more,
At five they say they will marry!

I once knew a sweet girl named Sybil
Whose surname was strange – it was Chibbel:
She hated the name,
So the first man who came
She married, and is Mrs Kabibbel.

There was a young fellow from Diss
Who asked his girl for a kiss:
'There'll be no sweet kisses
Until I'm a Mrs;
I won't kiss while I'm still a Miss.'

There was a young lady of Bow
Whose speech was exceedingly slow.
She married a guy,
And do you know why?
She was just too slow to say 'No'!

There was a young lady of Filey
Whose courting was clearly quite wily.
She met a laddie
Whose name was Paddy –
Now hers is Mrs O'Reilly.

Wedding day

A bright-eyed and lovely young bride
Said to the groom at her side,
'I'm happy and gay,
But nervous today,'
And the groom sat right down and he cried.

For his wedding, a very late suitor
Rode into church on his scooter.
He knocked down the Dean,
And said, 'Sorry old bean,
I ought to have sounded my hooter.'

The old Bishop of Bath and Wells
Married a pair of musical swells.
The bride's brother, Gordon,
Played on his organ,
And the bridesmaids were all wedding belles!

What noise at the wedding of Lynn!
Confetti was thrown in the din;
And also some rice,
Which would have been nice –
Except it was still in the tin!

Married life

I once knew a young girl from Suva
Who was an elegant mover.
The grace of her carriage
Led straight into marriage,
And she's elegant now with a hoover.

The husband of Geraldine Teaser
Found that he just couldn't please her.
When she asked him to do,
Just one chore or two,
He broke the fridge and the freezer.

A man wanted desperately to marry me,
And promised me riches if I'd agree.
Now that I'm his wife
I live the high life –
In a top-flat bed-sit in Hackney.

A newly-wed bride from Slough,
Admitted she didn't know how
To cook or to clean;
But her husband was keen
And he said, 'I'd better learn how.'

A slovenly chap called Jock
Had a big hole in his sock.
His wife said, 'Darn it.'
And then left for Barnet
With a similar hole in her frock.

I said to my wife, 'Dear spouse,
Be quiet and more like a mouse.'
Her answer to that
Was, 'You're just a rat,
So don't tell me what to do – louse!'

A thoughtful husband named Marvin,
Purchased a big joint for carvin'.
He took up the knife
And said to his wife,
'This joint will keep us from starvin'.'

A saucy young wife called Mabel
Sent her rich hubby a cable.
It read, 'Dear Sir,
I can't get fur;
Send money to me for a sable.'

A lonely widow named Kate
Was hardly content with her fate;
But she had a plan
To catch a new man,
And make him her second-best mate.

Any Distinguishing Features?

Inhuman

There now lives a man in Perth,
Who had a very strange birth.
His ears kept on growing,
His eyes are both glowing;
Could be he's not from our Earth.

A forester living in Stoke
Is not quite a human bloke.
The size of his thighs
Is quite a surprise,
For they're made of ebonized oak.

I know a man called Calhoun
Whose belly is like a balloon.
He is dark, not fair,
And he's covered with hair
And looks just like a baboon.

A man was given a drug
To improve his ugly mug.
His appearance is rare
With a face that is square –
Just like a Toby jug.

There was a young lady from Cheam
Whose face caused her boy-friend to scream.
He'd kiss her in the dark,
And just for a lark,
He once gave her vanishing cream.

An ugly old man in Perth
Said he would give the earth
For a girl who replied
She would be his sweet bride –
Instead of dissolving in mirth!

The monster from Mars is quite horrid:
His clothes are ill-cut and so florid,
His legs number three,
I'm glad he's not me –
His face has no nose and no forehead.

A monster said with a shrug,
As he gave his girl a big hug,
'I'm getting a replacement,
In fact a refacement,
My dear, for my ugly mug.'

There was a young man of Dumfries
Who had the most knobbly knees.
If he went to the park,
He'd go in the dark,
For dogs often mistook them for trees

A man from the Martian race
Has a peculiar face.
In place of ears
He had long spears,
But that's not so strange in space.

How unusual

There was a young man of Devizes
Whose appearance was full of surprises:
His nose was askew,
Only one eye was blue,
And his ears were quite different sizes!

My big brown eyes number four;
My mouth is compared to a door.
But my face I don't mind it,
For I am behind it –
I'm sorry for the people before.

A woman named Mrs Jane Simms
Gave birth to adorable twins.
She had great hopes
They wouldn't be dopes;
They weren't – but each had ten limbs.

There once was a young man called Steven
(This really takes some believin'),
Who used a peg
To lengthen his leg
When finding the ground was uneven.

You mucky pup!

A fancy-dress woman named Carol,
Dressed in the strangest apparel:
A hand-knitted coat
Made with hair from a goat,
And a frock in the shape of a barrel.

There is a boy called Chad,
A most untidy lad.
His hands are inky,
His clothes are stinky,
And his breath is awfully bad.

There's a woman in London called Gertie,
Who's just reached the prime age of thirty
Without using soap –
Unlike you, I hope.
That Gertie is – *phew* – really dirty!

There was a young boy from Leith,
Who hated to clean his teeth.
His dirty face
Was a real disgrace,
But he was a charmer underneath.

There is a fat sloppy man,
Who calls himself Peter Dan.
His beard needs trimming,
His belly needs slimming –
For Pete's sake, do what you can.

A man from Inverness
Always looks a mess.
His shirt is torn,
His jacket's worn,
And his trousers need a press.

There now lives a fellow called Stan,
A very peculiar man.
His beard needs trimming,
His body needs slimming,
And his skin could do with a tan.

A wife told her fat, dirty hubby:
'I don't mind you being so chubby;
But try to be seen
Looking slightly more clean.
I hate it when you look so grubby!'

There was a young man called Bertie,
Who was nearly always dirty.
Only his mum has the power
To induce him to shower;
It's disgraceful at his age – he's thirty!

Weighty problems

There is a fat girl named Lena;
Just wait until you've seen 'er.
She's like a big ball,
With no waist at all;
And a laugh just like a hyena.

A flabby young girl called Valerie
Is starting to count every calorie.
She'll no longer eat
Bread, fish or meat;
In time she'll be gone – no more Valerie.

There was a young lady called Lynn,
Who was so uncommonly thin,
That when she essayed
To drink lemonade,
She slipped through the straw and fell in.

There was a young fatty called Tim
Who was exceedingly dim.
He fasted for weeks,
And now rarely speaks.
He's wasting away, but he's slim.

A girl who was certainly stout,
Said with a bit of a pout:
'I must stay inside,
For the door's not so wide –
That's why I never get out.'

There once was an old queen of eighty
Whose problems were excessively weighty.
She weighed twenty stone
And damaged her throne;
And the king said, 'Watch it there, matey.'

> There was an old lady from Dorset,
> Who couldn't quite do up her corset.
> Eased with lard,
> The job was still hard,
> And the only chance left was to force it.

There was a young cook called Lyn
Whose boyfriend was terribly thin.
One day for some fun,
Whilst making a bun,
She used him as a rolling-pin.

> A lady who couldn't be fatter
> Insisted: 'It just doesn't matter.
> I'm going to eat
> All of my meat
> Fried and with plenty of batter!'

A girl who weighs many an ounce
Used language I shall not pronounce,
Her brother one day
Pulled her chair right away –
'Cos he wanted to see if she'd bounce!

> There was a young boy called Kevin,
> Who was most unusually thin.
> But he could be of use,
> Should your knickers come loose
> You could use the poor boy as a pin.

There was an old person who cried,
For he was so exceedingly wide.
At a restaurant he'd eat
All his meals on the street,
For he couldn't get in, though he tried.

> There was a fat lady of Rhyl,
> Who always consumed her fill.
> She put on weight
> Whenever she ate
> Her favourite meal – mixed grill.

There was a young man from Hackney
Who measured six feet round the knees.
He went down to Harwich
Nineteen in a carriage,
And found it a terrible squeeze.

> There was a young lady named Nelly
> Who had an enormous fat belly.
> In the hot sun she'd bask,
> And her neighbours would ask,
> 'What's there in Nelly's big belly?'

There was a fat lady called Hetty,
Who ate too much cream and spaghetti.
She kept getting bigger,
Like a full-masted rigger,
And she's now anchored close to a jetty.

A man by the last name of Gast,
Went on a twenty-day fast.
He grew so small
They can't see him at all –
All of his friends are aghast.

A very big girl called Kate
Wanted to learn how to skate;
But down at the rink
She started to sink,
When the ice cracked under her weight.

There was a young lady from Pinner
Who daily grew thinner and thinner.
The reason was plain:
She slept out in the rain,
And was never allowed any dinner.

There once was a fellow called Stan,
With a waist of remarkable span,
Said he, 'The odd inch
Is likely to pinch,
I must lose ten stone if I can.'

The long and the short of it . . .

There was a tall girl called Frankie,
Who when she dropped her pink hankie,
Tried hard to retrieve it,
But at last had to leave it –
Because the poor girl was too lanky.

A soldier (excessively short),
In battle successfully fought:
For cannonballs sped
Right over his head,
And one he actually caught!

Why doesn't little Paul
Leave his cap in the hall?
He said to Meg:
'I saw the peg,
But really I'm just too small.'

There was once a young man of Gibraltar
Who daily got shorter and shorter;
The reason, it's said,
Was the bag on his head,
Which was filled with the heaviest mortar.

Beautiful . . . well, almost!

There was a young boy at our school
Who's a hit with the girls as a rule.
He has but one eye
To ogle them by,
But it's massive and shines like a jewel.

There was a young lady named Sue
Whose eyes were a lovely blue.
She was a real cutie
And would have been a beauty –
If only her eyes numbered two!

A freckle-faced girl named Dot
Used to worry a lot.
She'd scrape her skin
With a very sharp pin,
And now she's down to one spot.

There was a young girl called Meg,
Whose pride was her one shapely leg.
The other leg's knee
Was amusing to see –
It was just like an egg on a peg!

Headlines

There was a young girl called Poppy
Who wore a hat far too floppy.
When it was in place
It quite hid her face –
Which wasn't necessarily a bad thing!

There was an old man called Ted
Whose nose was always so red:
Though you'd hardly know
For it didn't show,
'Cause all of his head's quite red!

A skinhead, Jimmy McBaines,
Dresses in studs and chains.
His head is quite bare,
He shaves off his hair –
Some claim he's without any brains!

There was a young man called Ed Hurly,
Who got to the barber's shop early:
By 9.15
He was as bald as a bean,
And his nickname was no longer 'Curly'.

There once was an artist named Pott,
Who seemed to have hair, but had not.
He wore a hair-piece,
Which he slicked back with grease
And tied on top with a knot.

Eye to eye

An odd-looking girl from Devizes
Had eyes of two different sizes.
One was so small,
It was no use at all;
But the other won several prizes.

There was a young girl called Nelly,
Who was always watching the telly.
Her eyes grew square;
But she didn't care,
So they packed her off to Pwllheli.

There was a young lady of Flint
Who had a most horrible squint.
She could see the whole sky
With the uppermost eye,
Whilst the other was reading small print.

There was a young girl called Sue
With beautiful eyes of blue.
One's made of soft glass
(Too bad for the lass) –
But no one can tell of the two.

There was a young girl, Mandy Figg,
Whose eyeballs were terribly big.
They grew so tremendous,
She looked quite horrendous
And closely resembled a pig.

Noses of note

There was a young man from Kent
Whose nose was terribly bent.
One day, I suppose,
He could follow his nose,
And no one would know where he went.

There was a young lady called Rose,
Who quite deliberately chose
To have no job
And be a snob –
Which suited her turned-up nose.

There was a young man known as Claud,
Whose nose could not be ignored.
When he blew his wide konk,
He let out a great honk,
Which could often be heard abroad!

There was a young lady of Pynn
Whose nose nearly reached to her chin.
The lady's quite poor
(She's also a bore).
That long-nosed young lady of Pynn.

There was a young girl called Rose,
Who had a large wart on her nose.
Her parents approved
When she had it removed,
But her glasses fell down to her toes.

I know of a woman called Rose,
It's no surprise that she goes
As far as she can
From any young man
Who shouts, 'You have a big nose.'

A guy with a very long nose
Was annoying a sweet girl named Rose.
She smashed on his konk
A bottle of plonk –
To get the bouquet, I suppose!

There was an old man of Montrose
Who had an enormous red nose.
His nose could be seen
From near Aberdeen,
If he stood on the tips of his toes.

My sister called Rose (who is older)
Has a nose that is bigger and bolder.
She can do a good trick:
Using it as a stick,
She can tap you on the shoulder.

There was a young lady named Rose,
Who had an extremely long nose.
She bent over low,
And what do you know –
Her nose could touch all of her toes!

Footnotes

There was a young lady of Fleet,
Whose shoes were too tight for her feet.
She couldn't walk
Or hardly talk:
Too bad – they looked so sweet.

There is a young boy called Pete
Who has unusual feet.
They turn out so much,
The heels only touch
But the toes – they never shall meet.

There was a young man from Cork
Who had a peculiar walk.
He'd stumble and fall,
Creep and then crawl,
Whilst people around him would gawk.

Medical Notes

Under the weather

A man from Mozambique
Surely must be unique
With a temperature mate
Of one hundred and eight –
But he hotly denies he's a freak.

An airline pilot called Lou
Was not sure of what to do.
She had a bad cough
When due to take off,
But finally flew with the flu!

I feel a chilly breeze;
It's colder by degrees.
My throat is sore,
And what is more,
I think I have to sneeze.

There was a young man from Deal
Who had a pain in his heel.
He had to go
On tippytoe,
And sometimes had to kneel.

There was a young man called Ted
Who baked some horrible bread.
He cooked large brown rolls
Filled with wide holes,
So now he's quite sick and in bed!

My friend is down in the dumps;
She's covered all over with lumps.
It could be, of course,
Acquired from her horse –
A true case of galloping mumps!

A young schizophrenic called Carruther,
Who, when told of the death of his mother,
Said, 'Yes, it's too bad,
But I can't feel too sad –
After all I still have each other.'

Sick humour

There was a young lady called Jane,
Who was dreadfully sick on a train.
Not once, but again
And again and again –
And again and again and again.

There is a young lad from York,
Who loves eating crispy, burnt pork.
He'll eat it so thick,
Till he's awfuly sick –
So thick that he can't even talk!

There was a young girl called Jill
Who travelled abroad to Brazil.
She ate soft, sweet toffee,
Hard nuts, and drank coffee –
Which all made Jill terribly ill.

There was a young lady of Twickenham,
Whose boots were too small to walk quickenham.
She bore them awhile;
But at last, at a stile,
She took them both off and was sickenham.

There was a young lady, Lucy,
Who loved a day out by the sea.
She drank a large beer
On Southend pier,
And was extremely sick after tea.

Home-cures

In the Arctic, a wonderful wizard
Got a fierce pain in his gizzard.
So he drank wine and snow
At fifty below,
And farted a forty-day blizzard.

A little boy from Kew
Had itches through and through;
But if he'd scratch
The ones at the back,
In front they'd start anew.

There was a blind man from Madeira
Who suddenly saw things much clearer.
For he found with surprise,
If you opened your eyes
Everything seemed so much nearer.

An Irishman named Doyle
Applied hot caster oil
To a wart on his neck.
He screamed, 'By heck,
This oil's been brought to the boil.'

An Englishman, John Bull
When dressing himself's no fool.
He knows that a chill
Could make him quite ill –
So he covers himself with warm wool.

A flu-ridden man named Bill
Put his head under the grill.
He turned up the heat,
Which cooked his own meat,
But also got rid of his chill!

There was a young man named Ted
Who had sore feet which bled.
His wife rubbed onions
All over his bunyons,
And both of them wept in bed.

A lady who lived in Peru
Was looking for something to do.
She took a cold shower
Every half hour,
And ended up with bad flu.

If you suffer from chills
Don't take any pills,
But very hot showers
For twenty-four hours:
This treatment cures you, or kills.

There was a young lady of Rhyl,
Who was exceedingly ill.
She made the assumption,
It was galloping consumption,
And she died from eating a horse pill.

Doctor's rounds

A New York lady called Joyce
Said in her real Brooklyn voyce:
'If you're feeling quite ill,
I can give you a pill;
For you see, I'm a fully-fledged noyce.'

A doctor named Andrew McLoffin
Said to a man who was coughin':
'It isn't the cough
That carries you off;
It's the coffin they carry you off in.'

There is a young surgeon from Sitges
Whose hard work is amassing him riches.
He now makes big money
By being quite funny
And keeping his patients in stitches.

A Frenchman from Aquitaine
Fell down a Parisian drain.
When fished from the river,
He'd damaged his liver,
And a doctor declared him in Seine!

The pain in my neck was a boil,
Which made the doctors recoil.
When the lancing was finished
My neck had diminished,
And my head's now held on by a coil.

A man who sleeps in the rain
Has just seen his doctor again,
Who knowingly said,
Whilst examining his head,
'You've water from rain on your brain.'

The Drinks are on Me

I have a young brother called Ken
Who's in trouble with daddy again,
For drinking rough cider
With Rosie and Ida:
These chums are only aged ten.

'Don't drink whiskey,' said Father,
'It ain't good for your brain.'
But I didn't have one to start with,
So I emptied my glass yet again.

I know a young man who's wiser
After failing the breathalyser.
At the end of the year,
He's giving up beer
In favour of coke and Tizer.

A happy young sailor called Sam
Was off on a trip to Siam.
The trip had embarked
When the captain remarked,
'You're drunk.' Sam replied, 'That I am.'

There was a young man called Andy,
Who liked to drink lemonade shandy.
A pint of the stuff
Was more than enough
To make his straight legs go bandy!

A merry young girl called Mandy,
Asked out to a pub by Andy,
Said: 'I don't really drink;
Just gin when it's pink,
And maybe a spot of dry brandy.'

An Irishman sent his daughter
To fetch a jug of strong porter.
She had a quick drink,
And turned a bright pink,
And that's how her father caught 'er.

There was a chef called Terry
Who came from Londonderry.
His Irish stew
Was popular, owing to
A sauce made of port and sweet sherry.

Spanish tourist, Jerry,
Drank a lot of sherry.
He got quite ill
In old Seville
And came home in a beret.

A friend of mine named Bruce
Wisely drinks just juice.
When he has sherry,
He not only gets merry
But turns to all shades of puce!

There was a young lady called Win,
Who ordered a gin at an inn.
The waiter said: 'No –
You'll have to go;
The drinking of gin is a sin.'

Dapper Dan of Derry
Loves his glass of sherry.
Each day he'll pour
A little more,
Until he feels quite merry!

A drinker down in Kerry
Started acting merry.
He said, 'My wine
Is mighty fine;
It's made from elderberry.'

There was a young man called Peter
Who gulped down wine by the litre.
At a restaurant in Rhyl,
They totalled his bill
By fitting him up with a meter!

Pint pots on bars in Gillingham
Have bartenders good at filling 'em;
And customers who,
After a few,
Are equally good at spilling 'em!

A shaky old man named Jim,
Filled his glass to the brim.
When proposing a toast,
I noticed that most
Of his wine was spilt over him.

There was a teacher, Don Dippled,
Who constantly drinking got tippled.
His class started rippling,
When asked if he liked Kipling,
He said, 'I don't know, I've not kippled.'

Law and Disorder

A policeman when out on the beat,
Helped a lady to cross the street.
As he lifted his arm
He said, 'You'll come to no harm,'
Then a lorry ran over his feet.

      There was a young girl of Tobago,
      Who was tortured for not eating sago.
      They stretched her back
      Upon a long rack
      And cured her of her lumbago!

A shop-lifter living in Tooting,
Was once discovered looting.
'You haven't a chance,'
Yelled police sargeant Glance,
'Give up or we'll begin shooting.'

      A copper who came to arrest us,
      With questions constantly pressed us:
      'Now, who started the fire
      And tell me why're
      You dressed in suits of asbestos?'

There was a policeman in Crete
Who walked the length of his beat.
Thiefs were appalled –
It took no time at all
Because of the size of his feet!

      A florist whose first name was Don,
      Was happy when the sun shone.
      But one day he was robbed,
      And he sobbed and sobbed:
      'I've been burgled, my flowers are gone.'

There is an old man named Gus
Who's making one hell of a fuss.
His automobile's
Been robbed of its wheels,
And now he must travel by bus.

      My brother Rob ignores
      All the rules and laws.
      He tells our pa
      His pinchings are
      Gifts from Santa Claus!

I know a young man who's a lout;
Instead of talking he'll shout.
He'll steal, never buy,
He's dishonest and sly,
And all of his words I would doubt.

      There was a young lad called Bob,
      Who Fagin taught how to rob.
      The lad's really proud
      Of his work in a crowd,
      And he's just got a job with the mob!

A boy from Hampton Court
Thought he'd have some sport
With Aunty Alice,
At Buckingham Palace,
And poured castor oil in her port.

A boy catapulted a stone
At the window of neighbours who moan.
But, hitting a tree
It came back, you see,
And shattered one of his own!

A man called Sidney Hersifal
Was tried by old Judge Percival.
What luck he had –
Though Sid is bad,
Percival is merciful.

A man, whose last name was Brock,
Had stolen a valuable clock.
He was captured I fear,
Then strapped in a chair –
Poor Brock was in for a *shock*.

There was a young man called John Frank,
Who was punished for being a crank.
As you can't change your socks
Once placed in the stocks,
By the end of the week his feet stank!

A thief was placed in jail,
His father put up bail.
When he got out,
The dirty lout
Quickly left by rail.

There was an old man named Max
Who owed the government tax.
He had to admit
It was quite a bit,
As he posted the money in sacks.

Maud

There was an old lady named Maud
Whose bank balance constantly soared.
For she rented TV's,
Then *sold* them; now she's
About to be locked up for fraud!

There was an old lady named Maud,
Who was really a bit of a fraud.
She sold *home-made* honey,
For a great deal of money,
To a poor unsuspecting man, Claude.

A rich businessman of Khartoum
Does well from the big tourist boom.
He sells quite a mix
Of trinkets and bricks
That he claims come from Pharoah's great tomb.

A certain young man of Brixham
Woos the women, then tricks 'em.
When he sees they have rings,
 Or valuable things,
He underhandedly nicks 'em.

A motorist called Justin
Discovered loads of rust in
A car that he bought
From a friend who he thought
He could have the utmost trust in.

An inventive thief is MacDaw,
Here's what he stole a sack for:
To fill it with looty
And all sorts of booty –
Then he scarpered right out of the door.

An unlucky crook called Paul
Decided to climb a high wall.
Once he had risen,
He saw just a prison,
With nothing worth pinching at all!

You've heard the story of Honest John,
Who went on a trip to the Parthenon?
He was chased by police
For disturbing the peace,
And he ended up running a marathon.

A daring woman called Flo,
Who swam in the river Po,
Was considered a menace
By the people of Venice,
And had to be taken in tow.

Stealing a plate of roast beef
Eventually brings one grief.
The gravy trail
Can hardly fail
To lead the cops to the thief.

A boy who just had to have more,
Stole all kinds of apples galore.
He grew somewhat glum
When the cops told his mum;
For she really was shocked to the core.

A kid from Barnard Castle
Was a trouble-making rascal.
He sent a clock,
That went tick-tock,
To Downing Street in a parcel.

There is a young man called Bobby
Who collects hats for a hobby.
He goes to hotels,
Which cater for swells,
And pinches the hats from the lobby.

A man of high morals from Lyme
Had three wives at a time.
When asked, 'Why three?'
He replied, 'One's too twee –
And bigamy, sir, is a crime.'

There was a young man of Cologne
Who gave a stray dog a bone.
But he later confessed it,
When he was arrested,
The bone wasn't even his own!

She offered accommodation
To tourists throughout the nation.
But one whose bed
Was in the shed
Is sueing for compensation.

A shipbuilder from John O'Groats
Took to forging ten-pound notes –
A job which was
Essential because
Not one of his boats ever floats.

A motorist from Tooting
Disliked police re-routing.
They ran him in
For making a din,
Constantly tooting and hooting!

There once was a thief named Bowers
Who daily stole beautiful flowers.
He feels crime's divine,
It suits him just fine –
Besides, he can choose his own hours.

There was an old servant, Marmaduke,
Who swore he'd never harm a duke.
But he pinched a sword
From his lordship's hoard,
Then confessed, 'I did disarm a duke!'

The cops now have an alsatian
Locked up secure in the station.
If the dog got out,
There is no doubt
He'd bite every kid in the nation.

There was a young girl called Hilary,
Who wouldn't eat her celery.
They put her in the stocks,
And picked up stones and rocks
And pelted her in the pillory.

Excessive Behaviour

Over the top

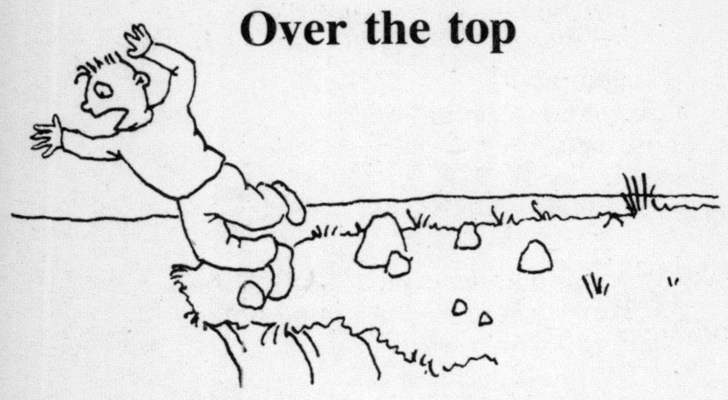

A boy who was Japanese,
Was far too anxious to please.
When asked to stay cool
For exams at his school,
He studied in the deep-freeze!

> A chatterbox named Kay
> Desired to have her say.
> Said she, 'Let us each
> Deliver a speech,
> And mine will take a full day!'

There was a young girl from Milan
Who wanted to learn the cancan.
She was ever so keen,
And her legs could be seen
Before the music began!

> A gambler, Maximilian,
> Who said he was Sicilian,
> Placed a bet
> Whilst playing roulette,
> And coolly lost a billion.

There once was a man called Hank
Who wanted to hold up a bank.
It couldn't be done
With just a small gun;
So he crashed through the doors with a tank!

> A mad engine-driver in Wales
> Frequently went off the rails.
> He'd drive his train
> Down small, country lanes,
> Flattening boys carrying pails.

There was a girl called Miss Cooper,
An expert hula-hooper;
But she wanted to fly
Across the sky,
And be a loop-the-looper!

> An angry motorist, Frank,
> Took all his cash from the bank.
> Now he happily slams
> Through all traffic jams;
> For he's bought himself a tank!

No exaggeration!

There was a young boy called Dan,
Who out shopping one day with Anne
Said: 'I cannot manage
To carry your baggage.
Why don't you hire a van?'

A tiny, young infant named Pam
Rides out in a very posh pram.
Silk linen lines it,
Ten nurses guide it –
Pam's pram was as big as a tram!

There was a young girl called Marge,
Whose frame was exceedingly large.
A canoe or small boat,
With her couldn't float.
What's needed, I fear, is a barge.

There once was a raw cadet,
Who knew little of etiquette:
So he learned how to talk
And eat with a fork
(Which the gardener hasn't missed yet!)

Excessively mean

There was a young lady called Liza
Who really was a miser
'Life's cheaper,' she said,
'When one stays in bed.'
So, she wasn't an early riser!

A girl with her hair in a tangle,
Thought she had found a new angle
For totally saving
On permanent waving,
By putting her hair through a mangle.

Said a miserly peer at the Abbey,
'Do you think that I look rather shabby,
For I've replaced my ermine,
Which was nibbled by vermin,
With the fur of my dear long-dead tabby.'

There was a young man called Shaun,
Who to save every penny was sworn.
So he learned how to sneeze
In various keys,
Thus saving the price of a horn.

There is a young man of Dundee
Who doesn't drink coffee or tea.
He'll sip a dry brandy,
Or even a shandy,
So long as he gets them for free!

There once was a man in the moon
To whom the stars were a boon:
His electric light
Wasn't needed at night,
Or even at dawn, or at noon.

There was a young man called Bert
Who lent his sister a shirt.
It was an extra-large size
And covered her thighs,
Which saved her from buying a skirt.

A man on the Aberdeen coast
Thought himself a good host.
He'd give you a bed
And even some bread –
Though it was usually yesterday's toast.

A housewife called Christina
Could hardly be much meaner.
She'll use a cat
To beat her mat,
Not a vacuum-cleaner!

There was a rich man, MacIntyre,
Who needed more fuel for his fire.
He tossed in the flames
His old butler, James,
Whose screams grew higher and higher!

There was a young lady of Rome,
Whose head was as bald as a dome.
Ladies beware –
She used to have hair,
Till she did her own perm at home.

A Scotsman known as Jock
Had a big hole in his sock.
He said, 'I knew
One toe had crept through,
But five – that's really a shock!'

Excessively shy

There once was an old man named Ted,
Who wasn't quite right in the head.
Whenever he saw
A girl at the door,
He'd crawl straight under his bed.

There was a young lady from Hayes,
Who went through a very shy phase:
Just like a mole,
She dug a hole
And stayed underground for three days.

Ill-Suited

or Unlucky for some

A trainee chef called Hugh
Wasn't quite sure what to do:
He was meant to thicken
His soup with chicken,
But instead used paste and glue.

There was a young man called Paul
Who decided to paper the hall.
From ceiling to ground
He papered around –
Now you can't see the doors at all!

A bullfighter, quite a charmer,
Is now a cattle farmer.
His career ended when
A bull entered the pen,
Dressed horn to hoof in steel armour.

There was a Scottish angler,
Who at fishing was a bungler.
Every last cent
On bait he has spent,
And now he is reeling with hunger.

An ample young Fraulein, Ms Fritz,
Is constantly dong the splits.
But this dancing act,
I'm afraid it lacks
The elegance seen at the Ritz.

There was a bus-driver, Rebecca,
Who came to be known as a wrecker.
When a bridge was too low,
She changed at one blow
From a double to a single-decker.

There was a young girl from Calais
Who wanted to join the ballet.
She didn't have a chance
For the way she'd dance
Was more suited to the local palais.

An unknown poet called Kleats,
Carved verse on garden seats.
The poems he scored
Were greatly flawed,
And most were just repeats.

Dan from Lancashire
Was a bank cashier.
A very hard worker,
He wasn't a shirker –
But quite a thief, I hear!

A science professor confesses:
'The secret of all my success is
Not the knowledge
I gained in college –
But simply some lucky wild guesses.'

There was a young man from Australia
Who tried to grow an azalea.
He nearly went crazy
When up popped a daisy –
What a horticultural failure.

An oriental chef called Ali
Works below decks on a galley.
His Bombay duck
Was poisonous muck,
So the crew flung him off at Bali.

There was a young gypsy in Welling
Who loudly declared she was selling
Her round crystal-ball,
Announcing to all,
'There's no future in fortune-telling.'

There once was a naval tailor,
Whose face grew visibly paler
When told transparent jute
Would definitely not suit
For the bell-bottoms of a sailor.

An old lady who lived by the park
Is burgled a lot after dark.
Her dog's an old pet,
But she really should get
Another that can at least bark.

A travelling salesman called Ray
Hardly knows the correct thing to say.
He's so unsure,
He'll knock on your door
Then rapidly run away.

A girl loved rock and roll
As well as blues and soul.
She'd listen to pop
Whilst at work in a shop,
So now she's on the dole!

A school ma'am of Herne Bay
Came to teach one day.
The boys all nattered,
The girls all chattered –
The teacher soon turned grey.

There was a young man from Greece,
Who decided to join the police.
He's kind-hearted and so
He lets the crooks go –
And crime has begun to increase!

There was a young man in Bengal
Who rented himself a small stall.
He tried to sell stamps,
Antiques and some lamps,
But he could sell nothing at all.

There was a young girl named Polly,
Who had a pet dog – a collie.
A champion sleep-dog –
But as a sheep-dog
It certainly was a wally!

A man with a business in Brecon
Is completely unable to reckon.
He thinks four plus four
Is sixteen or more:
His are the bills you should check on!

A kitchen assistant named Tessa
Balanced some plates on the dresser.
When she sneezed, they fell
And broke, sad to tell.
And oh, how the head cook did bless 'er.

A first-time flier, Pete,
Achieved an unusual feat.
He took off from Rome
For Gatwick and home,
But landed instead in Crete!

There was a young poet aged twenty-three,
Who, although he could trill like a linnet, he
Could never complete
Any poem with feet,
Saying, 'Idiots,
Can't you see
That what I'm writing
happens to be
modern
poetry?'

An angler now is wishing
He was at home and dishing
Up fried plaice
To feed his face –
He's caught no fish while fishing.

There once was a young man called Jake
Who tried to bake a soft cake.
He had no lard
And found it hard –
So do his teeth as they break!

An apprentice put marge on the cutter,
Which made the gardener mutter:
'But you said I must
Put grease on the rust,
And I didn't have any butter.'

There was a young woman called Ruth
Who had a large hole in her tooth.
She went to a dentist
Who was an apprentice –
He used a gun to shoot out that tooth.

A student, Edmund Kale,
Wanted to go to Yale.
He took a test
And did his best;
But the results made Edmund pale.

A decorator called Max,
Who fixes sheds and shacks,
Is very much faster
For he doesn't use plaster –
Just papers over the cracks!

In Cardiff, an aircraft designer
Took off in the lightest air-liner;
But easterly gales
Swept across Wales,
And took him to North Carolina.

Once I fell asleep in a bunk,
On a Chinese boat called a junk.
But when I awoke
I'd had a good soak,
For in Shanghai harbour we'd sunk!

A pigeon living at Euston
One day flew as far as Houston.
His wings were so tired
He nearly expired,
But still there was no perch to roost on.

At the countdown a bold astronaut
Thought that Mission Control had said 'Nought.'
But that hero's Zero
Was just a mis-hear, so
He orbited more than he ought!

A certain young lady named Iris
Now knows what a very flat tyre is.
She had to pay
To be towed away,
And soon learned how dear a car-hire is.

A long distance driver from Dunbar
Proceeded north but didn't get far.
He drove away
On a hot, sunny day,
But his wheels got stuck in the tar.

A yachtsman by the name of Walter,
Assayed to sail around Gibraltar.
But he lost his way
One stormy day,
And wound up on the island of Malta.

There was a playful, young Greek
Who liked to play hide-and-seek.
He hid under a bed,
In the garden shed,
And hasn't been found for a week!

I know a girl called Ada,
Who says it's never paid 'er
To put coins in slots,
As not one of her shots
Has brought down a Space Invader.

There was a girl called Honey
Who owned a cute, pet bunny.
It nibbled her purse;
But what was far worse,
It ate up most of her money!

There was a young man from Bengal,
Who was asked to a fancy-dress ball.
He said he would risk it
And went as a biscuit –
But a dog ate him up in the hall!

There was a young man from the Humber
Who finds it quite hard to slumber.
He's counting white sheep
In order to sleep –
And he's up to a million in number!

There was an old farmer in Spain
Who misguidedly prayed for rain.
The resultant showers
Lasted for hours,
And washed his farm down the drain.

I went to the hut of old Jack
And knocked on the door round the back;
But the slightest shaking
Starts his house quaking,
And now it's a tumbledown shack.

A girl in Alice Springs
Had some water wings.
But in a drought,
There is no doubt
They're pretty hopeless things.

There was a young girl named Yvonne
Who bathed in the river Don.
But a terrible drought
Gave her reason to shout:
'Where's all the water gone?'

There once was a young man called Burton,
Who was told of a horse that was certain
To win the big race,
Or at least get a place;
But the horse came in last – poor old Burton.

There was a young man called Neil
Who went round on the big wheel.
But halfway around,
He looked to the ground –
Which cost him a fifty pence meal.

Travellers' Tales

Ship, plane, car, train.

There was a huge creature on Mars
Who had two pedal-cars.
Each of the things
Had a pair of sleek wings
And he used them to travel the stars.

There was a young man called Terry
Whose nose was as red as a berry.
Had he been on a cruise,
Or drunk too much booze?
Both – on the Woolwich ferry!

A fast young man called Murray
Drove in a tearing hurry
From Hampshire to Kent,
And remarkably spent
Only ten minutes in Surrey.

A fussy young girl called Lorraine,
Decided to travel to Spain.
She said, 'No trips
In planes or ships –
I'll only travel by first-class train.'

There was a young man called Gordon
Who stupidly went abroad on
A day return
To Rome and Berne,
Through Istanbul and Jordan.

A traveller on a cruise to Quebec
Stayed up all night long on deck.
He got wet through and through
When a raging storm blew,
And he entered the port a sea-wreck.

There was a train traveller called Hugh,
Who missed the last train to Crewe.
At the station in Dundee,
He went for a pee,
And locked himself in the loo.

Destination unknown

There was a young man of Quito
Who wanted to see Hirohito:
But in Ecuador,
Geography's poor,
So he went to Belgrade and saw Tito.

I once knew a girl, Clementine,
Who rode on a train to the Rhine.
How did she feel
When she arrived in Keele?
She must have got on the wrong line.

Sight-seeing

A Scottish lake's called a loch –
And here's a bit of a shock.
A highland king
Has drained the thing
And sold it as a dry dock!

I knew a girl named Tinx
Who went to visit the sphinx.
I asked, 'Dear Tinx,
How is the sphinx?'
Said she, 'I think it stinx!'

There was a young girl from Carlisle,
Who holidayed on the Nile.
But swimming was out,
When she spotted the snout
And the smile of a large crocodile!

That man should take a bow,
He's learned Red Indian now.
He studied each night
To get it quite right –
It's easy when you know 'How'!

There once was a young man called Warren
Who put on a kilt and a sporran.
When he got to York,
On the Pennine Walk,
Everyone saw he was foreign!

There was an old lady of Greece,
Who went on a tour with her niece.
'It's not like back home,'
Said she when in Rome,
'For they have such handsome police.'

There was a young man called Roland
Who went on a trip to Poland.
There were blizzards all night –
The morning turned white,
And Poland looked just like a snowland.

A traveller from Lake Tana
Took a trip to Ghana.
He brought a packed lunch
To quietly munch,
Of three dates and one ripe banana.

A specialist on flowers
Studied them for hours –
In Zanzibar
Where pansies are
Only grown in showers.

I walked for hundreds of miles
Throughout the great British Isles.
Upon reaching Dover,
I'd nearly climbed over
More than two thousand stiles!

A South African by the name of Carl
Decided he must leave his kraal.
He went on safari
Across the Kalahari,
Then rented a flat in Transvaal.

A man who retired to Tibet,
Worked up in the hills as a vet.
He treated the backs
Of overworked yaks –
How low (or how high) can one get!

In the hills of Indonesia
Is grown the flower called a freesia.
It needs a good blow,
And there as you know
The weather is often much breezier.

National characteristics

An Irishman called Shamus,
On 'Mastermind' is famous.
He quite outclasses
The others with 'passes' –
My God, what an ignoramus.

A Red Indian tribe, the Siouxs,
Wore neither trousers, socks nor shoes.
It may seem queer
Thus to appear –
But what you ain't got you can't lose!

They snooze in the heat in the East
After lunch for three hours at least;
There's complete inertia
Throughout all of Persia,
And all that will rise is yeast.

People north of the Tweed
Are Scotsmen, it's agreed.
From the lowlands or highlands,
The mainland or islands –
On porridge and haggis they feed.

There was a young girl called Sonia
Who met a guy in Bologna.
She wondered was 'e
Perhaps an Aussie?
For he often said, 'Good on yer!'

An Indian queen's called a rani,
And wouldn't there be a barny
If one of them said:
'I'd rather be dead
Than have to learn Hindustani.'

If you are a Hindu
The cow is sacred to you.
To show respect,
You genuflect
Each time you hear it moo.

There was a fakir named Brian,
Who wanted a hard bed to lie on.
He went to a store
And ordered a score
Of nails and long pieces of iron.

In Frankfurt a man called Herr Hermann
Can speak in both English and German.
His accent's so thick
That poor Uncle Dick
Can't determine the words of Herr Hermann.

Coming home

A man who went to Hong Kong
Stayed there a wee bit too long.
Back home now, in Pinner,
He can't start his dinner
Till somebody beats on a gong.

There is a young man from the Bronx
Who hasn't been home now for yonks.
He really does yearn
For a hero's return,
With ticker-tape, sirens and honks.

Exit

These'll kill you

A silly boy named Hyde
At a funeral was spied.
When asked, 'Who's dead?',
He laughed and said:
'Who knows? I'm just here for the ride.'

'Sorry I'm late,' said Pa,
'The cemetery was quite far.'
His concerned daughter said,
'Why, is anyone dead?'
He answered, '*All* of them are!'

A lad who dyed cotton in Lancs
Was always engaging in pranks;
One day, sad to say,
He tripped in his play
And died in his own dyeing tanks.

There was a professor called Hock,
Who invented a marvellous lock.
He tried it on his door
And was trapped for a week or more,
And he never got over the shock.

A restless young lady from Tyne,
Sat on a very large mine.
She thought 'twas a dud 'un,
But it went off sudden –
She can now be in ten places at a time.

A pure-natured woman in white
Told Arthur, a tall, handsome knight,
'To prove I adore you,
I'd die darling for you.'
She was buried that very same night!

There was an old man of the Tyne
Who was almost completely blind.
One day it was found
He'd gone underground,
When he unfortunately fell down a mine.

Arty, a vegan from Neath,
Announced with his dying breath,
'It's healthy to eat greens,
Raw cabbage and beans . . .' –
Poor Artychoked to death!

There was a young fellow from Tyne,
Who put his head on the Northern line.
But he died of ennui,
For the 5.53
Didn't come till a quarter past nine.

There was a poor moggie from Hyde,
Who heard that the dog next door had died.
He went through the gate,
And met a terrible fate,
'Cause the cat that had told him had lied!

A man with his head in a noose
Struggled to work himself loose.
His moves made it tighter,
His face grew much whiter,
Said he, 'I'll be hanged – it's no use.'

A bachelor without any hope,
Decided he just couldn't cope
With not being matched;
So he calmly attached
Himself to the end of a rope.

An old lady who came from Kilbride,
Ate so many apples she died!
The apples fermented
Inside the lamented,
Making cider inside 'er inside!

A cat who tragically sighed,
Decided upon suicide.
She passed under the wheels
Of eight automobiles,
And after the ninth one she died.

Deep in the woods is a baby deer,
Lost from his mummy and cold I fear.
While looking to play
He strayed far away,
And soon he'll be no more, the poor dear.

At a precipice there's a hush,
In Alaska, just after a rush
Of dogs and sledge
Over the ledge –
For someone had shouted out, 'Mush!'

Missing

A very fat man from Boston
Went to a river and crossed on
A bridge that was weak,
Which spanned a creek;
And that was the trip he was lost on!

An angler from Belvedere
Lost all of his fishing gear
(Including his hook),
When he stupidly took
A long walk on a very short pier!

There was a young man in Wales
Who didn't care much for the dales.
He got his thrills
From the highest hills,
Until blown away by strong gales.

There was a young man of Gloucester,
Who had a sweet girl, but then lost 'er.
Down a small country lane,
He found her again,
In a hedge where a bull had tossed 'er!

There was a young man named Ron,
But nobody knows where he's gone.
He sat on this chair,
Now he's simply not there;
Well, it did have a rocket strapped on!

A timid zoo-keeper named Ben
Entered a fierce lion's den
On tippy-toe
A week ago,
And hasn't been seen again!

There was a young lady of Ayr,
Who went to the local funfair;
She let go her hold
Of the swing-boat I'm told,
And was suddenly no longer there.

A certain young couple from Kent
Camped out on a hill in a tent.
A big storm one day
Blew the couple away,
And nobody saw where they went.

There was a young girl called Sally
Who drove in a big motor rally
On a mountain route
She failed to hoot,
And speedily arrived in the valley!

Dead stupid

There was a young fellow named Vivian
Who had a dear friend, a Bolivian,
Who dropped his cigar
In a gunpowder jar,
And blew himself into oblivion.

A driver named Jonathon Master
Stepped on the gas to go faster.
Just for some thrills
He flew over the hills,
And ended in total disaster.

There once was a chief of the Sioux,
Who into a gun-barrel blew
To see if 'twas loaded.
The rifle exploded –
As he should have known it would do!

A chemistry student called Myrna
Was not an intelligent learner.
By a gas-filled jar,
She smoked a cigar,
Lit from a bunsen burner.

Killer instinct

There was a young doctor called Hyde.
To a patient he did confide,
'My real name is Jekyll,
But don't you dare heckle;
The ones who have tried it have died.'

A handsome young gent from Florida
Collapsed in a hospital corrider.
A young nurse from Maine
Sought to banish his pain,
And shot him. Now what could be horrider?

There was a small boy from Redruth
Who pushed his small mum off the roof.
When he was asked why,
He just gave a sigh,
And remained completely aloof.

A youthful beef-packer named Young,
One day when his nerves were unstrung,
Pushed his wife's ma, unseen,
In the chopping machine;
Then canned her and labelled her 'Tongue'.

Man-eater

A missionary, Father O'Ryan,
Tried to teach hymns to a lion.
How could this be?
It must be that he
Is quite looking forward to dyin'.

There was a young lady of Riga
Who went for a ride on a tiger.
They returned from the ride
With the lady inside,
And a smile on the face of the tiger.

A girl from the equator,
Brought up an alligator.
It seemed like a friend,
Until in the end
It opened its jaws and ate 'er!

There was a young lady called Pat
Who sat with a cat on a mat
When along came a Puma –
An over-consumer –
That was the end of the mat, the cat and Pat!

There was an explorer called Ada,
Who travelled to the equator.
She disappeared,
And now it's feared
That an alligator ate 'er.

A lovely little alligator
Lived quite close to the equator.
For lunch it might eat
A child's head for its sweet,
And save what was left for later.

A hungry fish, a piranha,
Gobbled up a girl called Dana.
Now, this was a shame,
For she'd acquired some fame
And was soon to tour around Ghana

Zany Humour

A future of automation
Should fill us all with elation,
Especially the shirkers
And unhappy workers –
For we'll be an unemployed nation.

'The city of Bucharest
Is different from Budapest:
The Danube flows through
Them both, it is true;
Now I'm slightly confused,' he confessed.

A foolish young girl called Amanda
Didn't know a male goose was a gander.
She was given a bear
Full of stuffing and hair,
And thought it a real living panda!

A short-sighted lady called Rose
Could not see to the end of her nose.
She lived all alone
In a world of her own,
Which is not a bad thing I suppose.

A set of twins aged ten
Wished to be nine again.
So they picked the lock,
And turned back the clock,
And swore they would never be men.

I knew a man named Ivor,
Who was a deep-sea diver.
A shark he met
Said, 'I'm in debt –
Please will you lend me a fiver?'

The punishment for a traitor,
Devised by a nasty dictator,
Is a week in the lake
Which – not by mistake –
Contains a huge alligator.

The lifeboat that's kept at Torquay
Is intended to float in the suay.
The crew and the coxswain
Are sturdy as oxswain,
And as smart and as brave as can be.

There was a young lad from Bristol,
Who understood, clear as a crystal,
That someone would get
Exceedingly wet
When he shot off his big water-pistol.

There once was a loud brigadier,
Who was fond of ten thousand a year;
When he heard the guns rattle,
He'd cry, 'To the battle!' –
Then discreetly sneak back to the rear.

A generous man named Mick
Sells ice cream on a wood stick.
If you haven't enough
To buy the cold stuff,
He'll charge you a penny a lick.

I once knew a lady called Jane,
Who was always disposed to complain,
'This is no good,
That is no good.'
Everything she would disdain.

There was a young girl called Ruth
Who never could tell the truth.
When she began to complain,
'My mouth's full of pain,'
The dentist yanked out the wrong tooth.

My friend who is called Tony,
Is such an incredible phoney.
He bought a Great Dane,
Which he led by a rein,
Pretending that dog was a pony.

A bossy young fellow called Jeff
Just got a job as a chef.
If he finds some gristle,
He'll blow a loud whistle,
As if he's a copper or ref.

There was a young man named Nicose
Who lacked pockets in all of his clothes.
There's no place for money
Which might appear funny,
But Nicose says, 'That's how it goes!'

A hairy young fellow named Bryan
Forever was cryin' and sighin':
'Do you think that my shape
Was derived from an ape?
Well I think Charles Darwin was lyin'.'

The admiral of the fleet
Gave himself a treat.
He went afloat
In a rubber boat
And rowed from Rome to Crete.

Said Mrs Isosceles Tri,
'That I'm sharp I've no wish to deny;
But I do not dare
To be perfectly square –
I'm sure if I did I should die!'

There once was a dubious priest,
Who lived almost wholly on yeast.
For he questioned what was said,
That our spirits rise once we're dead,
And he wanted to get started at least.

That stuck-up fellow, Vince,
Could really make you wince.
He's such a snob,
He's got a job
As a boot-licker to a prince.

A cultivator of cactus
Very unjustly attacked us:
He said, 'You're all spineless;
And what's more you're mindless.'
He then sold his cactus and sacked us.

Down on the River Exe
Divers search for shipwrecks.
It isn't for leisure,
They hope to find treasure,
But not in the form of cheques.

There was an old man from Carlisle,
Who sat down one day on a stile.
The paint, it was wet,
So he's sitting there yet;
But he hopes to get off with a file!

A smart mermaid of Stockholm
Each day on her hair used a comb.
To clean her tail,
She'd stand on a whale
And shower 'neath his jet of foam.

Why did Uncle Jim
Look so horribly grim?
He didn't know
The music show
Was simply hymn after hymn.

A wild beast is the boar,
Bad-mannered and what is more,
He'll knock down huts
To get at nuts
And eat them right off the floor.

There was a man in Jarrow
Who grew a giant marrow.
To no one's surprise,
It won the first prize –
But crushed a vegetable barrow!

There was a young girl called Susanna,
Who marched in a parade in Havanna.
She wobbled indeed,
So no one could read
The words printed on her bright banner.

I have a friend called Harrison;
It's disgraceful how she carries on.
She goes to school,
To fight and fool –
Why, I'm demure by comparison.

A sailor who came from Bombay
Got ill in the Bay of Biscay.
'I'm not feeling well,'
The sailor would yell;
But now the poor lad's ok!

There was a young lady of Hove
Who sat down by mistake on a stove;
When they asked, 'Is it hot?'
She replied, 'It is not,'
Said they, 'She's a tough one, by Jove!'

There was a young man from Tralee,
Who was stung in the neck by a wasp.
When asked if it hurt,
He said, 'Not a bit!
It can do it again if it likes!'

There was an old man of Calcutta,
Who had an unfortunate stutter.
'I would like,' he said
'Some b-b-b-bread
And some b-b-b-b-b-b-butter.'

There was a young man of Kent
Who couldn't pay all of his rent;
Because of that,
He left his flat,
And now he sleeps out in a tent.

A vintner of Tunisia
Never had been busier.
He makes champagne
From grapes and rain,
Because he claims it's fizzier!

There was a young man named Hugh
Who thought that his blood was blue.
The cheeky young pup
Was so damn stuck-up
That his blood more likely was glue.

A certain school-girl called Madge,
Who was always on the cadge,
Had 'MAY I BORROW
UNTIL TOMORROW',
Printed, in caps, on her badge.

I once knew a couple of louts,
Who now have become good boy scouts.
One of them, Reg,
Grows his own veg,
Known in the town as 'boy's sprouts'.

There was a young lady of class,
Who wanted her house filled with brass.
She said to Jemima,
'Just an egg-timer
Is all that I want made of glass.'

There was a young boy from Bengal,
Who played with his pink rubber ball.
He threw the ball high,
Way up in the sky,
But it never came down, not at all.

The handsome vicar of Bray
Saw a skunk who was passing his way.
The skunk gave a squirt,
So the smell's on the shirt
Of the vicar, who said: 'Let us pray.'

A farmer now living in Stoke
Slept with his pigs for a joke.
His wife had a fright
When she joined him that night,
And smelly at dawn, they awoke.

A boy who told tall tales
And made some shady deals,
Became too bold
With a bike he sold
That didn't have any wheels.

An ancient people, the Huns,
Are said to be the ones
Who spread the news
Of public loos –
They must have had the runs!

A kid by the name of Bo Diddle
Practised for hours on his fiddle.
His mum always bakes
Him cookies and cakes,
And he's growing quite wide in the middle.

A woman whose last name was Brite,
Had very bad dreams in the night.
Each noise that she'd hear
Caused pangs of great fear,
And she'd shuddder and shake with fright.

A pregnant girl called Nelly,
Sat in front of her telly
Eating a pear,
Whilst washing her hair,
And scratching her big bulging belly.

The Isle of Man agrees
Its parliament, hidden by trees,
Is burglar-proof;
And this is the truth,
For they call it the House of Keys.

A man who lived in Khartoum
Was ordered to use his new broom.
This housewifely sweeping
Was unhappily keeping
The man from his knitting and loom.

A man with two mackintoshes,
Through dismal slush he sloshes.
But his feet are wet,
So he'll have to get
Some wellies or galoshes!

By waving his magic stick,
A conjuror did a trick:
He made a box
Of sweets and chocs
From what had once been a brick.

Daily life is confusing
And really not very amusing.
Machines are robotic;
The traffic's chaotic;
So I simply avoid it by snoozing.

A short Chinese woman called Mingaling
Loved talking and trying to singaling.
She adored cuckoo clocks,
Their ticks and their tocks,
And bells that went tingaling, dingaling.

There was a man who supposed
His open front door was closed.
So a thief big and bold
Strolled in, stole his gold,
Whilst that foolish old man dozed.

There was a young lady of Hull,
Who was charged by a virulent bull;
But she picked up a spade,
And yelled, 'I'm not afraid,'
Which distracted that mean, vicious bull.

There was a young man named Josh,
Who talked a whole lot of bosh,
In cultured tones
With moans and groans,
And tried to sound very posh.

A WOMAN WHOSE LAST NAME WAS BRITE...

There once was a brown and white duck
Who one day was down on his luck.
When a hunter's gun fired
That poor duck expired,
For that dumb bird forgot he should duck.

> There was a young lady called Pat
> Who liked to stop for a chat.
> She'd rather talk
> Than quietly walk –
> Though Pat often talked through her hat.

There was a young man of Kings Lynn
Who said, 'I don't think it's a sin
To bet on a horse,
Provided, of course,
The gee-gee comes in with a win!'

> Asked a young man, Roger Willoughby,
> 'What can a feather-filler be?'
> I said, 'In bed,
> Something soft for your head –
> Elsewise, what would a pillow be?'

A lady who disliked the rhumba
Wanted to hear a new number.
She said, 'Please play
Something quite gay,
But quietly so I may slumber.'

> There was a young man from Cheam
> Who in anger let out a loud scream,
> For his trouser leg
> Got caught on a peg
> And split quite in two down the seam.

Said one of the girl-friends of Peter
(Who keeps his pets near a heater)
'Is that a wart-hog
A dingo or dog?'
He said, 'Can't you tell an ant-eater?'

> A fellow who came from Tennessee
> Trained a tiny, performing flea.
> An insect which
> Can make you itch –
> Eeek! It's just jumped onto me!

There was a young girl called Heather
Who wasn't afraid of the weather.
She'd say, 'The rain
Is no longer a pain
Now that I'm clad in leather.'

> Among the birds of South Harrow
> Dwelled Tina, a tiny young sparrow.
> The bird quickly grew,
> And one day off it flew –
> That sparrow's now gone from South Harrow

I know a young sailor called Duncan,
His buddy is Solomon Bunkin.
Both dive to their boat,
Which simply can't float
Because it is totally sunken!

There was a lad called Dave
Who fell into a cave.
He cried and cried
Until he died –
Dave wasn't very brave.

There was a young lad named Len
Who'll never be one of the men.
He's like Peter Pan
And knows that he can
Never be older than ten!

There is an old lady of Norwich
So poor that she has to forage
For something to eat –
She'd much prefer meat
But may only wind up with porridge.

There was a young laddie called Dave,
Who with fervour and vigour did crave
For some hair on his chest
To poke through his string-vest,
And some stubble so that he could shave.

Young Barry was very gymnastic,
His suppleness was quite fantastic.
To pick his nose
He'd use his big toes –
His limbs were attached by elastic!

On the bridge stood Mary Chiver,
Her lips were all a-quiver;
She gave a cough,
Her leg fell off
And floated down the river!

A cameraman in Frome
Fitted a lens called a zoom.
He could see Big Ben
Striking quarter to ten
Without even leaving his room.

There once was a dinosaur, Jake,
Who would eat nothing but cake.
But it hadn't been invented
So he grew thin and dented,
And how his poor belly did ache!

A very important mayor
Opened an antique fair.
The reason was
Just because
He was the oldest thing there.

I once saved a guy from drowning –
A man renowned for his clowning.
'I'm just the man
If you need a tan –
My name is Frederick Browning.'

At the Sports Committee, Stan,
A most athletic man,
When discussing the mile,
Thought for a while,
Then stood up quickly and ran.

There was a young slave called Christina,
Who ran from a Roman arena,
For the lions were prowling,
And hungrily growling,
And couldn't have looked any meaner.

There was a young baker called Ned,
Whose bank account was in the red.
Said the manager there:
'Your larder is bare;
You've got to get hold of some bread.'

An expert on birds went to Auckland
Desiring to see a big hawk land.
But all he saw
Were pigs galore,
So he renamed the area Porkland!

There was a young student called Fred,
Who hadn't a thought in his head.
He couldn't have a brain
For he seemed quite insane,
And he looked to be totally dead.

There was a young swimmer called Mark
Who, when he spotted the fin of a shark,
Said, 'I'm not keen on dying;
I'm taking up flying!'
So he did and flew off like a lark.

In bed I think I shall stay,
Instead of working all day.
I'll sleep and I'll dream
Of cherry ice-cream,
And bright flowers that bloom in May.

Tall stories

There is a young man from Kentucky
Who nicknamed his girl-friend 'My ducky';
She answered him back
With a quick 'Quack, quack, quack',
Then gave him a peck, which was plucky!

An expert on wild birds
Claims that about two-thirds
Of nightingales
In southern Wales
Can sing their songs with words!

Have you ever seen a ghost?
I have, while I was eating my toast!
It came through the wall,
Amazing us all,
And said: 'Tell me, which way to the coast?'

There was a young man called Herman,
Who claimed that he spied a *merman*.
If it seems to you
This tale's not quite true,
Remember it's translated from German.

A mighty hunter, Baboo,
Had fought a dragon or two.
He'd give them a punch,
And then he would lunch
On the meat of a fine dragon stew!

There was a boy called Dick,
Who could do a clever trick.
He'd eat sand and water,
And plenty of mortar,
Then regurgitate a brick.

A lady from Tipperary
Swore that she spied a fairy:
A little gnome
With a balding dome,
And a chin that was horribly hairy.

An old man who managed a farm,
Viewed his bullock with growing alarm;
For wings it grew,
Then up and flew
Away from that old man's farm.

There was a young lady of Hanley
Who found herself growing manly.
At first she faltered,
But finally altered
Her name from Stella to Stanley.

There was a young man called Russell,
Whose body was filled with big muscle.
But during a rag,
He dressed up in drag
And danced a slow waltz in a bustle!

I knew a man called Morris
Who had a wife named Doris.
Just as he feared,
She grew a beard –
So now he calls her Horace.

There was a young woman from Looe
Who dreamt she was eating her shoe.
She awoke in the night
In a terrible fright,
To find it was perfectly true.

There was an old man of Nepal,
Who had a most terrible fall;
He was split quite in two,
But by using strong glue
They mended the man of Nepal.

Dan, Dan, an ugly old man,
Had a wash in a toilet pan.
He combed his har
With the leg of a chair,
And admired his face in a frying pan.

There once was a man from Stour
Whose knuckles were terribly sore.
He'd been knocking all day,
And his hair had turned grey,
But still no-one answered the door!

A boy walked down a long road,
At a leisurely pace he strode.
He signalled a car –
'Slow down 'cause you are
Driving too fast on this road!'

> A lad who often gardened
> Really has to be pardoned
> For breaking a spade.
> It was, I'm afraid,
> Because the ground had hardened!

A good-looking youth named Hector
Wanted to be a rector,
The bishop said 'No –
You'll just have to go
And first be a ticket inspector.'

> A beaver by the name of Sam
> Got himself into a jam
> 'Cause he would sun
> With work half done –
> He simply didn't give a dam!

A man from the Appalachians
Breeds the best dalmatians.
He knows that their spots
Appeal to lots
Of people from all generations.

> The vicar said, 'I see that Hugh
> Is once more missing from his pew.
> Now let us pray
> For those astray,
> And hope that Hugh is in the loo.'

There was a young girl, Annette,
Who wanted to join the smart set.
Her casual dress
Was a suitable mess
And her poodle was just the right pet.

> An old English coin, the groat,
> May be found in a castle's moat.
> This fourpenny piece
> Could buy many geese
> Or perhaps a secondhand boat!

A girl with poor speech, known as Button,
Enjoys eating bloody raw mutton
Without any spice –
She claims it tastes nice,
'I love eatin' mutton with nuttin'.'

> Patricia could not have been grimmer –
> She felt she could have been slimmer.
> I said, 'But Pat
> You're not too fat
> To be a strong channel swimmer.'

A maths teacher with a long beard
To all of his students declared,
'I'll see if your knowledge
Is ready for college –
By testing how well you've prepared.'

I know of two MD's
Who caught a rare disease.
It made them freeze
And cough and sneeze –
The cure was cottage cheese.

A couple called Bonnie and Clyde
Went for a motor-car ride.
They held up a bank
(It wasn't a prank)
Then drove off in order to hide.

There was an old man of Woking
Who gave his fire a good choking.
It made so much smoke
That the local folk
All started coughing and choking.

A very strange thing is a newt –
It seldom, if ever, eats fruit.
It dwells in ponds
Living on fronds
And says not a word – it's mute.

Ealing comedies

There once was on old man of Ealing,
Who had an expectorant feeling.
But a sign on the door,
Said DON'T SPIT ON THE FLOOR,
So he looked up and spat on the ceiling.

I know of two fellows in Ealing,
Who pace back and forth on the ceiling.
They walk upside down,
Without looking round
For no reason – they just like the feeling!

A pious priest from Ealing
Always prays whilst kneeling.
He helps the poor,
And what is more
He cares, and works with feeling.

There is a young man of Ealing
Whose sun-tan is constantly peeling.
This loss of skin
Makes him look thin;
What he needs is a total wax sealing.

A fashion-conscious bather from Ealing
Wore a G-string – most revealing.
When he jumped in the sea
It got wrapped round his knee,
Which afforded a sight quite appealing.